CONTENTS

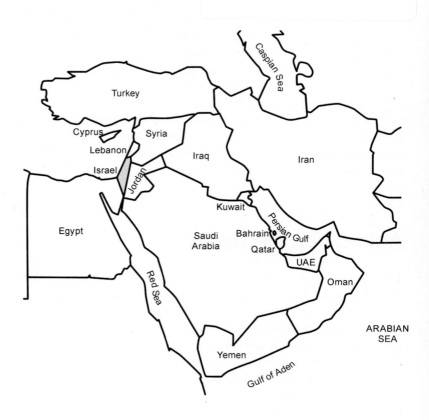

Helion & Company Limited
26 Willow Road, Solihull, West Midlands, B91 1UE, England
Tel. 0121 705 3393
Fax 0121 711 4075
Email: info@helion.co.uk   Website: www.helion.co.uk   Twitter: @helionbooks   Visit our blog http://blog.helion.co.uk/

Published by Helion & Company 2015
Designed and typeset by Kerrin Cocks, SA Publishing Services
Cover designed by Kerrin Cocks, SA Publishing Services
Printed by Henry Ling Ltd, Dorchester, Dorset

Text © Shlomo Aloni 2015
Monochrome images sourced by the author
Colour profiles drawn and commentary written by Tom Cooper, © Tom Cooper 2015
Maps drawn by George Anderson © Helion & Company Limited 2015

Cover: Photograph - Squadron 101 pilot Zorik Lev flew Mystère 43 to interdict SPINACH on the morning of 2 November 1956.
Aircraft profile - This Mystère IVA was originally slated to enter service with another unit; this aircraft (serial number 6684) received very large serials applied in black on the forward fuselage, but also complete campaign stripes. It is shown as in configuration for attack on Ras Nasrani on 2 November 1956, armed with pods for seven unguided rockets calibre 68mm, when it was shot down by Egyptian AAA. The pilot ejected safely and was recovered by a Piper from No. 100 Squadron shortly afterward.

ISBN 978-1-910294-12-3

British Library Cataloguing-in-Publication Data.
A catalogue record for this book is available from the British Library.

Note

One of the most important virtues of an officer is credibility. A military organization supposedly cannot win a war without credibility along chain of command. It is therefore assumed that most –- surely not all – debriefs are credible, so whenever possible this presentation of ILAF operations during the 1956 Suez War prioritizes debriefs and contemporary reports over accounts from biographies, interviews and memoirs. Unfortunately, many ILDF and ILAF debriefs and reports have not been unearthed yet so this presentation of ILAF operations, mostly from an Israeli perspective, along the timeline of the Suez War, is not fully complete and not absolutely accurate; but it is the best possible effort at this point in time.

Shlomo Aloni

1 February 2014

Acknowledgements

This presentation of ILAF operations during the Suez War benefits from materials that have been gathered over a timeframe of more than 20 years from national archives and personal collections; the author wishes to express special gratitude to ILDA staff members Doron, Ifat and Shirli, as well as thanking Oded Abarbanell, Jacob Agassi, Hagy Agmon, Moshe Aran, Dalya Ash, Zvi Avidror, Dror Avneri, Yigal Bar Shalom, Dan Barak, Asaf Ben-Nun, Israel Ben-Shahar, Michael Ben-Josef, Isaac Biran, Amnon Bloch, Isaiah Bodilewski, Moshe Bokai, Judah Borovik, Elyashiv Brosh, Shlomo Carmel, Cheetah Cohen, Brian Cull, Arie Dagan, Uri Dekel, Leslie David Easterman, Yoav Efrati, Jonathan Etkes, Achikar Eyal, Eli Eyal, Ron Feldman, Arie Fredilis, Elisha Galon, David Gatmon, Isaiah Gazit, Josef Gideoni, Shabty Gilboa, Abraham Goldreich, Albert Grandolini, Reuben Harel, Johnny Harris, Achiya Hashiloni, Leif Hellstrom, David Helman, ILPO, David Ivry, Mati Kaspit, Shabty Katz, Gideon Kohen, Zvi Lavon, Amity Levin, Ruth Livneh, Gideon Magen, Judah Manor, Ovadia Nachman, Nathan Navot, David Nicolle, Haim Niv, Josef Ofer, Dave Orli, Arie Oz, Eldad Paz, Moshe Peled, Amos Peleg, Akiva Pressman, Haim Proshanski, Arie Raviv, Yael Rom, Asher Roth, Meir Ruff, Yossi Sarig, Mordechai Segal, Noga Shadmi Lavi, Jonathan Shahar, Samuel Shamir, Daniel Shapira, Zeev Sharon, Meir Sheffer, Samuel Sheffer, Amram Shemer, Gideon Shenhav, Rafael Sivron, Gabriel Strasman, Zeev Tavor, Yoash Tsiddon, Ran Yahalom, Uri Yarom, Zahik Yavneh, Arie Zeelon, Adam Zivoni and Levy Zur for documents, memories and photos; all presented photos originated from collections of the aforementioned.

Glossary

AAA	Anti-Aircraft Artillery
AGL	Above Ground Level
AIR3	ILAF Air Department third branch (operations)
AIR4	ILAF Air Department fourth branch (intelligence)
ALO	Air Liaison Officer
AMV1	*ARAB MiGs, Volume 1*(2009), by Tom Cooper and David Nicolle
ASAP	As Soon As Possible
AUSTRALIA	ILDF code for Bir Hama
AUSTRIA	ILDF code for unknown locality but possibly a slip of the pen for AUSTRALIA
BDA	Battle Damage Assessment
CASEVAC	Casualty Evacuation
CAT1	Category 1 accident: no damage
CAT2	Category 2 accident: damage repairable at unit level
CAT3	Category 3 accident: damage repairable at depot level
CAT4	Category 4 accident: damage not repairable
CARROT	ILDF code for road along Abu Ageila/Bir Hasana/Mitle
CHAIR	ILDF code for road along Rafah/Ktziot/Quseima/Quntila
CYPRUS	ILDF code for Mitle Pass
EGAF	Egypt Air Force
EGDF	Egypt Defense Force (armed forces/army)
EGNF	Egypt Naval Force (Navy)
FAC	Forward Air Controller
FRAF	France Air Force
FRANCE	ILDF code for El Arish
FRNF	France Naval Force (Navy)
GLO	Ground Liaison Officer
HF	High Frequency (radio)
HOLLAND	ILDF code for Bir Lahfan
HQ	Headquarters
IFF	Identification Friend or Foe
ILAF	Israel Air Force
ILDF	Israel Defense Force
ILDF//G	ILDF General Staff Branch
ILDF//I	ILDF Intelligence Branch
ILNF	Israel Naval Force (Navy)
IOKB	ILAF Operation KADESH BDA Report
IOKR	ILAF Operation KADESH Research (February 1957)
JAMAICA	ILDF code for Battalion 890 drop zone east of Mitle Pass
JAPAN	ILDF code for Ruefa Dam Junction along SPINACH
JOAF	Jordan Air Force
JODF	Jordan Defense Force
MAT1	ILAF Material Department Branch 1 (Logistics Organization)
MAT2	ILAF Material Department Branch 2 (Engineering Maintenance)
MAT3	ILAF Material Department Branch 3 (Maintenance)
MAT4	ILAF Material Department Branch 4 (Engineering Design)
MAT5	ILAF Material Department Branch 5 (Ordnance)
MIOR	Mission Order (Hebrew letter representing month and numeral counter)
mph	miles per hour
OPOR	Operation Order
PEPPER	ILDF code for road along Quntila/Thamad/Nekhel/Mitle
PXNE	*Phoenix over the Nile, a history of Egyptian air power 1932-1994*–(1996), Lon Nordeen and David Nicolle

RADISH	ILDF code for road along Gaza/Rafah/El Arish'/Romani/Qantara
RTB	Return to Base
SEAB	Suppression of Enemy Air Bases
SEL	Single Engine Landing (in twin engine aircraft)
SPINACH	ILDF code for road along Quseima/Abu Ageila/ Jabel Libni/Bir Hama/Bir Gafgafa/Tasa/Ismailia
STOOL	ILDF code for road along El Arish/Abu Ageila/ Quseima
SYAF	Syria Air Force
SYDF	Syria Defense Force
TABLE	ILDF code for road along El Arish/Bir Lahfan/ Jabel Libni/Bir Hasana/Nekhel
TOT	Time On Target
USSR	Union of Soviet Socialist Republics
VHF	Very High Frequency (radio)
WOSZ	*Wings Over Suez* – Brian Cull with David Nicolle and Shlomo Aloni

Brief Background

Israel won the 1948 War and subsequent Arab terminology emphasized aspirations for a 'second round' war that would eliminate the disgrace of Arab defeat in 1948. Egypt – as leader of the Arab nations – sponsored terror activities against Israel and blocked international sea lanes to Israeli ships. Hostilities between Egypt and Israel, and a Middle East arms race, intensified from the autumn of 1955 but did not result in war because both Egypt and Israel avoided escalation. Key milestones during the deterioration to war were Egyptian statement on 11 September 1955 that practically closed the Straits of Tiran to Israeli shipping, the arms deal between Egypt and the USSR that was made public on 27 September 1955, and the Egyptian President's announcement of the Suez Canal's nationalization from its Anglo-French owners. The first milestone gave Israel a *casus belli*; the second milestone motivated Israel to launch a preventive war before Egypt would receive arms from the USSR; but only the third milestone actually enabled Israel to exploit an opportunity to implement three objectives: open the Straits of Tiran to Israeli shipping, destroy the Egyptian arsenal and deter Egypt from pursuing its policy of a 'second round' war.

Military Balance

AIR4 evaluation of the EGAF's order of battle on 29 October 1956 was:

Base	Unit	Type	Assigned Aircraft	Notes
Abu Sueir	30	MiG-15	15	plus Syrian squadron with 25 aircraft
Almaza	1	Fury	8	a flight
	3	Il-14	20	
	7	C-46	20	
	11	C-47	25	
	?	Meteor	6 night fighters	squadron No unknown, only two active crews
	-	Vampire	15	reserve aircraft

Base	Unit	Type	Assigned Aircraft	Notes
	-	MiG-15	70	50 assembled in storage plus 20 being assembled
Cairo West	8	Il-28	12	being organized
	9	Il-28	12 plus 6 Lancasters	with 5 more Il-28s in reserve
Fayid	2	Vampire	15	
	5	Meteor	12	
	20	Meteor	10 plus 20 Vampires	conversion unit
Kabrit	15	MiG-15	15	
	?	MiG-15	10	conversion unit, squadron No unknown
Kasfareet	31	Vampire	15	wartime recce revealed that Kasfareet was actually inactive
Luxor	?	Il-28	20	AIR4 did not elaborate but probably in storage

AIR4 also evaluated the number of EGAF pilots at 40 MiG pilots, 30 Vampire pilots, 10–15 Meteor pilots, 16 Il-28 pilots and 50 transport pilots, plus 10–20 pilots assigned to staff duties. For comparison, IOKR's eve-of-war order of battle – although not wholly accurate – is presented with the addition of two columns: squadron commanders and known ILAF numbers:

Unit	Type	Aircraft	Commander	Known ILAF Numbers
69 (1)	B-17	3	Jacob Ben Haim	1621 1622 1623
100	Piper	30	Michael Keren	0401 0402 0416 0421 0431 0432 0434 0437 0438 0440 0443 0444 0445
				0446 0447 0448 0449 0450 0451 0452 0453 0454 0455 0456 0459 0466
				0467 0468 0469 0470 0471 0472 0473 0474 0476 0484 0490 0492
101	Mystère	37	Benjamin Peled	4528 4529 4530 4533 4535 4542 4543 4544 4545 4546 4547 4549 4550

Unit	Type	Aircraft	Commander	Known ILAF Numbers
				4552 4560 4561 4562 4563 4564 4565 4580 4584 4585 4590 4591 4592
				4593 4594
103	C-47	19	Jacob Avisar	1401 1402 1403 1404 1405 1406 1407 1408 1409 1411 1412 1414 1416
				1418 1420 1422 1424 1426 1428 1430 1432
	Noratlas	3		4X-FAQ 4X-FAR 4X-FAS
105 (1)	P-51	15	Moshe Tadmor	2310 2319 2324 2325 2326 2328 2331 2333 2335 2336 2339 2354 2359

Unit	Type	Aircraft	Commander	Known ILAF Numbers
110 (1)	Mosquito	13	Ezekiel Somech	2117 2123 2124 (2126) 2133 2135 2167 2168 2169 2170 2171 2173 2174
				2175 2176 2177 2179 2181 2184
113	Ouragan	29	Moti Hod	4025 4026 4028 4029 4030 4041 4042 4043 4044 4045 4047 4049 4050
				4051 4052
115 (3)	Mosquito	2	Eli Eyal	2101 2132 2139 2178 2190 2191
116 (2)	P-51	19	Zahik Yavneh	2301 2303 2304 2306 2311 2312 2320 2329 2330 2332 2337 2338
				2343 2345 2351 2352 2353 2370 2373
117	Meteor	13	Aaron Yoeli	3515 3517 3518 3602 3603 3604 3605 3606 3609 3731 3733 3734 3735
				3737
119 (4)	Meteor	3	Yoash Tsiddon	3850 3851 3852
140 (2)	T-6	38	Moshe Eshel	1127 1128 1129 1140 1144 1153
147 (2)	T-17	35	Meir Sheffer	2713 2730 2731 2736 2748 2753 2755
	Consul			2811 2815 2816

The Suez War caught the EGAF amidst transition to USSR-made equipment; this MiG-15 was reportedly photographed at Abu Sueir between the start of deliveries - reportedly in October 1955 - and the Suez War, so the EGAF had an edge of up to six months in comparison to ILAF introduction of Mystère from April 1956.

The ILAF introduced Mystère from April 1956 so that by October 1956 there was only one squadron at Hatzor and aircraft for second squadron stored at Ramat David; these three Squadron 101 Mysteres - 4552, 4562 and 4563 - were photographed at Hatzor during the summer of 1956.

(1) Reserve squadron.
(2) Emergency squadron.
(3) Reconnaissance Squadron.
(4) Night Fighters squadron.

Due to permitted space, preparations for war, post-war unit reports, post-war statistical summaries and lessons from war are not covered – but hopefully will be presented in future titles covering ILAF operations in timeframes before and after the Suez War – as this book focuses on ILAF operations from the start of war on 29 October 1956 until the ceasefire on 8 November 1956.

Day 1
29 OCTOBER 1956

ILDF objectives for Day 1 were to preserve deception and surprise until H-Hour and to drop Battalion 890 over Mitle sector, a relatively short distance from the Suez Canal.

A Squadron 113 maintainer refuels an Ouragan at Hatzor; the Ouragan is painted with the first version of ILAF Suez War IFF stripes.

Squadron 140 deployed to tents at Teman Field, north-west of Beer Sheba.

SUEZ WAR STRIPES

MAT2 repeated, in a telegram that was circulated at 0420, an earlier order to paint IFF stripes on ILAF aircraft:

> Paint a stripe around the rear part of the fuselage, perpendicular to aircraft longitudinal axis, in between leading edge of the tail section and trailing edge of wing and around each wing perpendicular to aircraft lateral axis, halfway between wing tip and root. The stripe will be painted with two colors: center, 30 centimeters wide, in yellow; two edges, seven centimeters wide each, in black. Painting will start on the morning of 28 October [1956] and will be completed ASAP... This telegram refers to all aircraft in country and not only to ILAF aircraft...

The stipulated stripes were actually a variation of the ultimate Suez War coalition IFF stripes, primarily because at the time the coalition did not exist. Reference to *all aircraft in country* covered the arrival of FRAF aircraft; Tel Nof reported, at 0640, the arrival of 10 FRAF Noratlases.

ATTACHMENT TO ARMY

Squadron 100 – with the main body deployed from Ramla to Beer Sheba from 28 October 1956 – was tasked to assign four Pipers to Command South, one Piper to Division 38, one Piper to Division 77, one Piper to Eilat HQ and eight Pipers to Brigade 202; Phase B assignment was to be four Pipers to Command South, three Pipers to Division 38, one Piper to Eilat HQ, two Pipers to Brigade 9 and three Pipers to Brigade 202. At 0600, the flight commanders were reported: Division 38 Flight Commander, Zvi Armon; Division 77 Flight Commander, Josef Aaroni; Eilat HQ Flight Commander, Benjamin Kahane; and Brigade 202 Flight Commander, Isaac Hirsh.

SURVEILLANCE SINAI

	110	2167	Gatmon//Segal	patrol Mediterranean Sea
	110	2176	Orli	test
	110	2173	Shemer	Tel Nof –Ramat David
	110	2168	Orli//Kislev	patrol Mediterranean Sea
	110 #1of2	2177	Levin//Hy	patrol Mediterranean Sea
	110	2176	Proshanski //Dishoni	patrol Mediterranean Sea, RTB, SEL
	140	1127	Gideoni//Djaldetti	Beer Sheba – Tel Nof – Beer Sheba
	147	2736	Sheffer	training
	69	1622	Efrat//Narunski	training
0630–0700	101red1	4584	Gonen scramble to interception	
0630–0710	101red2	4590	Gur	ditto
0835–1145	115	2132	Tavor//Galon MIOR Yud128 photo air bases along Suez Canal	
0855–1155	115		Mosquito Yud132 photo Sinai coastline from Eilat to Sharm El Sheikh	Portugali
0900–1010	101 white1	4550	Bar Yud129 patrol for recce, fuel problem, RTB	
0900–1055	101 white2	4585	Bet On Yud129 patrol for recce	
0935–1105	101 white1	4529	Morgan Yud129 patrol for recce, replacement	

Squadron 110 maritime patrol missions were possibly related to Operation COCK that took place prior to the start of KADESH Day 1 events.

MIOR Yud128 photographic interpretation revealed 17 MiGs at Kabrit; eight MiGs and one Il-14 at Abu Sueir; 16 Vampires, eight Meteors and one Il-14 at Fayid; and no aircraft at Firdan, Kasfareet and Shalufa. The MiGs at Kabrit were dispersed and AIR4 reported that Cairo West was ordered, at 1300, to disperse aircraft. Traffic between Suez and Mitle was reported as sparse. Both Squadron 115 crews reportedly *sensed* EGAF aircraft in flight but AIR4 did not detect take-offs from Suez Canal air bases and Squadron 101 Mysteres were not vectored to engage.

READINESS STATE C

AIR3 ordered all units, at 0930, to prepare for Readiness State C, one level below war, from 1300. Instructions included:

> Aircraft dispersal from 1730; assembly of Squadron 160 (dummy) aircraft from 1730... blackout from 1730.

MONITOR MITLE

0935–1045	101 green1	4562	Nevo	reconnaissance Mitle
0935–1045	101 green2	4561	Lev	ditto

Israel undertook to pose a threat to the Suez Canal and the ILDF planned to position paratroopers west of Mitle Pass, some 30 kilometers east of the Suez Canal. The ILAF recced Mitle; by 0300 ILDF//I finished interpretation of the 28 October 1956 recce and concluded that EGDF troops were present west of Mitle, near the planned drop zone. Discussions continued until 0930, when the drop of dummies was canceled, and until 1000, when ILDF//G//Operations ordered a change of drop zone to east of Mitle; the new drop zone was some ten kilometers east of Mitle and five kilometers south-west of the Mitle//Bir Hasana//Nekhel road junction. It was therefore during discussions that Squadron 101 was tasked to fly visual reconnaissance over Mitle; pilots reported that the drop zone was clear of enemy forces.

STILL SINAI

1355–	117	Meteor	Lavon scramble to interception	
1355–	117	Meteor	Alroy	ditto
1415–1625	115	2101	Lavon//Dim	photo

Squadron 117 pilots were scrambled to intercept a radar track but found nothing. The Squadron 115 crew flew a largely uneventful mission over Sinai, the exception being the observation of an enemy jet flying between El Arish and Rafah.

CABLE CUTTERS

1500–1730	116	2373	Yavneh Yud120 cut communication	
1500–	116	2301	Hasson	ditto
1501–1726	116	2306	Barak Yud120 cut communication	
1501–	116	2329	Zeelon	ditto

The change of drop zone impacted the MIOR Yud120 cable cut mission that tasked P-51s to cut communication lines in Sinai at two points, along CARROT, from 1600. Yud120 stipulated a low altitude flight, radio silence except for an emergency and that pilots would make certain that the lines were indeed cut.

Following ILDF//G//Operations notification to AIR3, at 1200, about a shift to the east of the telephone lines cutting points, due to a change in drop zone, AIR3 issued, at 1235, a revision to MIOR Yud120: the former eastern first cutting point was transformed into

Squadron 116 pilots, standing left to right: Squadron 116 Commander Zahik Yavneh, Squadron 116 Deputy A Dan Barak, Squadron 116 Intelligence Officer, Cheetah Cohen, Arie Fredilis and Amnon Bloch; on wing left to right: Israel Burstein, Ami Hativa, Shlomo Geva, Squadron 116 Deputy B Arie Zeelon, Zvi Kohorn and Zeev Sharon. This photo was taken after 0600 on 2 November 1956 as P-51 is marked with ILAF Suez War IFF stripes version 2 and after 1700 on 2 November 1956 when a Squadron 100 Piper returned Shlomo Geva, with a bandaged forehead, to Tel Nof; Day 1 cable cutter missing from this photo is Amity Hasson.

Squadron 116 servicemen, most if not all reserves, turn around a P-51 during the Suez War; the cable cut P-51s were target tug equipped and were planned to cut cables with a long steel cable. This photo was taken after 0600 on 2 November 1956 as P-51 is marked with ILAF Suez War IFF stripes version 2.

the western second cutting point, while a new first eastern cutting point replaced the old western second cutting point. TOT over the first target was changed to 1545. Dan Barak recalled:

> Our mission was to cut lines in two places... My cable was detached during take-off so I had to land and mount another cable. We flew low and arrived over target. I took part in [pre-war] tests which were so classified that I did not know the purpose but there was one line between two poles over flat terrain and I cut it like butter. Suddenly, [there was] not one line but many lines and sand dunes so my cable was torn away. I remembered that an aircraft accidently cut lines with [its] propeller so I decided to do it [to cut the lines with the propeller]. I circled, signaled to my wingman to fly in line astern, descended [and headed to the lines] but at the last

In order to enable Squadron 103 to drop a battalion in one round trip, Israel loaned C-47s from France and these were issued with ILAF Numbers 1414 to 1432 in even numbers only; this image of 1418 - in which Squadron 103 pilot Yossi Ofer flew MIOR Yud118 on 29 October 1956 - was taken after its return to France but still with ILAF Number 1418 and still marked with ILAF Suez War IFF stripes version 2.

moment I instinctively pulled up. I tried again, fully fine so that RPM would be high, more than 2,000 RPM... and I sensed something like a black shadow for a split second. I circled to see [the] impact and could not find the place so I did it again... We flew to the second place... and did it again. Post-war we toured the area, not only [had] I cut the lines but I pulled out poles! ... on the way back we saw the paratroopers at the Mitle.

DROP MITLE

1520–1820	103	1414	Avisar/Rom/Eyal/Alon Yud118 drop Mitle
1520–	103	1416	Thor/Sela/ ditto Kovach/Menahem
1520–	103	1430	Bliman/Gil/ ditto Levanon/Malka
1520–	103	C-47	Navot/Rosin/ ditto Vronski
1521–1821	103	1418	Ofer/Lee/Zioni/Nimrod Yud118 drop Mitle
1521–	103	1402	Vossman/Ronen/ ditto Erez
1521–1831	103	1409	Ben Josef/Shapira/Harsit/ Toig ditto
1521–1821	103	1401	Shabty/Oz/ ditto Ashkenazi
1522–	103	1411)	Shalev/Biran/Shahaf/Sinai Yud118 drop Mitle
1522–1822	103	1412	Shamir/Peer/ ditto Ronen/Bok
1522–	103	1404	Ohad/Reubeni/ ditto Bahari
1522–	103	1405	Biham/Dvir/ ditto Shenar/Machnes
1523–	103	1420)	Yaffe/Vedeles/Ilani/Ben Ami Yud118 drop Mitle
1523–1843	103	1426	Biran/Barkai/ ditto Strasman
1523–1823	103	1424	Kohen/Richter/ ditto Cohen
1523–	103	1411)	Amrami/Michaeli/ ditto Dayan/Barnea

AIR3 issued, at 1025, MIOR Yud118 which tasked Squadron 103 to drop Battalion 890 east of Mitle at 1700. The stipulated altitude for the flight to the target was 5,000 feet AGL and 4,500 feet for the flight from the target. Aircraft unable to take-off on time and unable to arrive over the drop zone by 1720 were to take-off later for TOT at 2145, flying to and from the target at 4,000 feet.

Brigade 202, tasked to advance along PEPPER and link up with Battalion 890, crossed the border at 1600 and was thus the first Israeli force to set foot in Sinai; Battalion 890 followed from 1700 with each four-ship formation dropping a company, from 1,200 feet, over a drop zone that was – as concluded in a post-war inquiry – only three kilometers away from the planned drop zone. Drop dispersal was approximately 2,000 meters long and 500 meters wide; 13 paratroopers were injured during the drop but by 1930 Battalion 890 was organized in a defended locality east of Mitle.

ARMLESS DECOYS RAFAH QANTARA

1525–1615	115	3518	Eyal	Yud126	decoy
1525–1615	115	3518	Livneh	ditto	

MIOR Yud126 tasked Squadron 117 to launch two unarmed Meteor trainers to fly a decoy mission at 30,000 feet, along a route from Rafah to Qantara and back, from 1630 until 1720, in zigzag flight so that the average advance speed would be 140–150 mph. Squadron 115 Commander Eli Eyal and Squadron 115 pilot Meir Livneh flew the mission in two Squadron 117 Meteor trainers. ILAF post-war analysis of EGAF radar coverage concluded that the four Egyptian radar stations, active on 29 October, covered the north half of Sinai but were unable to track targets flying higher than 26,000 feet.

RELAY MITLE

1545–	103	1422	Ganot/Buchman/ relay Nahum/Voss

FAC Yekutiel Alon – radio call sign GIFT – dropped with Battalion 890. At the end of the drop, the C-47 captained by Amnon Amrami remained over the drop zone and established radio contact with GIFT; 1422 replaced Amrami at 1730 but was unable to contact GIFT.

FIRST PIPER TO MITLE

1545–	100	0447	Even support Brigade 202

Battalion 890 was planned to prepare a landing strip for Piper immediately after the end of the drop. In line with this plan, the first Piper departed Eilat at 1545, flew to Quntila and from there to Mitle. Moshe Even established radio contact with GIFT but was unable to land, since the landing strip was not ready. GIFT asked Even to recce the road from Mitle to Suez. No unusual activity was detected so Even headed back to Eilat, but was asked to land at Quntila for CASEVAC to Lod, from where Even flew to Beer Sheba.

ESCORT TO DROP ZONE

1600–	117	Meteor	Yoeli	Yud121 escort Squadron 103
1600–	117	Meteor	Sapir	ditto
1600–	117	Meteor	Altman	ditto
1600–	117	Meteor	Gat	ditto

1615–	117	3734	Zivoni	Yud122 escort Squadron 103
1615–1725	117	3604	Kaspit	ditto
1615–	117	Meteor	Ben Aaron	ditto
1615–	117	Meteor	Alroy	ditto
1615–	117	Meteor	Lavon	ditto
1615–1725	117	3605	Yahalom	ditto
1635–	113	Ouragan	Hod	Yud123 escort Squadron 103
1635–	113	Ouragan	Lapidot	ditto
1635–1735	113	4052	Agassi	ditto
1635–	113	Ouragan	Erez	ditto
1635–1735	113	4026	Kishon	ditto
1635–1735	113	4025	Ivry	ditto

MIOR Yud121 tasked Squadron 117 to escort Squadron 103 from 1620 until 1640. The four Meteors were to fly from Tel Nof to a rendezvous point at 30,000 feet, descend and split into two pairs, with one pair flying at 5,000 feet and the other at 10,000 feet.

MIOR Yud122 tasked Squadron 117 to escort Squadron 103 from 1635 until 1655. The six Meteors were to fly from Tel Nof to a rendezvous point at 30,000 feet, descend and split into two sections, a four-ship formation flying at 5,000 feet and a pair at 10,000 feet.

MIOR Yud123 tasked Squadron 113 to escort Squadron 103 from 1650 until 1710. The six Ouragans were to fly from Tel Nof to a rendezvous point at 25,000 feet, descend and split into two sections, a four-ship formation flying at 5,000 feet and a pair at 10,000 feet.

MIOR Yud121, Yud122 and Yud123 stressed:

Aircraft will intercept any enemy aircraft approaching airlifters.

PATROL KABRIT

1635–1740	101green1	4584	Peled	
	Yud125 patrol Kabrit 1650 to 1705			
1635–1740	101green2	4585	Egozi	ditto
1635–1740	101green3	4550	Bar	ditto
1635–1740	101green4	4565	Avneri	ditto
1636–1750	101black1	4562	Nevo	
	Yud125 patrol Kabrit 1651 to 1710			
1636–1750	101black2	4592	Lev	ditto
1636–1750	101black3	4533	Alon	ditto
1636–1750	101black4	4529	Morgan	ditto
1645–1755	101white1	4546	Shapira	
	Yud125 patrol Kabrit 1700 to 1719			
1645–1755	101white2	4545	Shavit	ditto
1645–1755	101white3	4552	Gonen	ditto
1645–1755	101white4	4561	Gilboa	ditto

MIOR Yud125 tasked Squadron 101 to patrol between Mitle and Kabrit from 1650 until 1719. Unlike the escorting Meteors and Ouragans, whose only ordnance was guns, the patrolling Mysteres had guns and rockets. The first formation was tasked to patrol at 10,000 feet; the second and third formations were to start their patrol at 30,000 feet and, after ten minutes, descend to 10,000 feet in order to overlap patrol watches at 10,000 feet. All three formations were to fly to and from the patrol station at 30,000 feet. MIOR Yud125 stressed:

Squadron 117 servicemen during deployment to Tel Nof. Standing on veranda, left to right: Uri Gat, Shabty Ben-Aaron, Shlomo Sapir, Yossi Sarig and Technical Flight Commander; sitting on floor of veranda: Nahum Yahalom; sitting on stairs, left to right: Hillel Alroy, Mordechai Lavon and Mati Kaspit.

Squadron 101 Mysteres with ILAF Suez War IFF stripes version 1 and rockets pods. ILAF Number of photographed Mystère possibly ends with 2; 4552, 4562 and 4592 flew MIOR Yud125 on 29 October 1956.

ILAF maintainers servicing a P-51 with ILAF Number last digit 8 - probably 2338 - at night. Nighttime was exploited to prepare as many aircraft as possible for next day operations.

Aircraft will intercept any enemy aircraft approaching airlifters. Aircraft will attack any fighter aircraft attempting to take-off from Kabrit. Aircraft will attack any vehicles advancing in direction of drop zone.

ESCORT FROM DROP ZONE

1650–	113	Ouragan Sharon	
		Yud124 escort Squadron 103 from 1700 until 1720	
1650–	113	Ouragan Rosen	ditto
1650–	113	Ouragan Bet On	ditto
1650–	113	Ouragan Zuk	ditto
1650–	113	Ouragan Har Lev	ditto
1650–	113	Ouragan Furman	ditto

FROM SUNSET TO MIDNIGHT

	100	0444 Lolav/Brigade 202scout	support Bde 202
	103	1403 Navot/Peer/ Vronski	drop Mitle
	103	1414 Avisar/Rom	drop Mitle
	103	1420 Oz/Dvir	Yud137
	103	C-47 Ohad	drop Mitle
	103	FAQ Thor	drop Mitle
	103	FAR Yaffe/Kohen/Eyal	
	Yud137 drop Mitle		
	203	Noratlas French/Goldreich	drop Mitle
2345–0445	103	C-47 Gil	relay Mitle

Sunset was at 1656; Brigade 202 reported the occupation of Quntila at 1717; Brigade 4 crossed the border at 1730. Squadron 100 reported, at 1900, that Pipers departed Eilat bound to Mitle for CASEVAC. Piper 44 became disoriented and landed somewhere in the desert, south-west of Abu Ageila.

At 1915 ILDF ordered the ILAF to avoid offensive operations for as long as the EGDF would not attack the ILDF. At 2000, Brigade 9 also crossed the border and reported the occupation of Ras Naqab.

Battalion 890 was dropped without equipment and supplies so MIOR Yud137 covered the drop of mortars, recoilless guns and crews as well as Jeeps and supplies; an ILAF navigator was teamed with each Squadron 203 French crew, primarily for communication and coordination; the drop of equipment and supplies started at 2100 and continued past midnight.

Roughly twice or three times a day, AIR1 prepared an ILAF order of battle table that was not wholly accurate but presented a fair picture of ILAF potential at the time of issue. The ILAF order of battle report for 2200 on 29 October was:

Base	Unit	Type	Serviceable for Combat	Serviceable for Flight	Notes
Ramat David	69	B-17	2	-	5 pilots, 4 navigators,
					3 radio operators, 17 gunners
	100B	Piper	-	2	
	105	P-51	9	2	15 pilots
	110	Mosquito	11	-	12 pilots, 5 navigators

Base	Unit	Type	Serviceable for Combat	Serviceable for Flight	Notes
Dov Field	119	Meteor	2 (night fighters)	-	1 pilot, 1 navigator
	128	Piper	2	-	9 pilots
		T-17	5	-	
Ramla	100A	Piper	-	7	3 pilots
		T-17	-	1	2 pilots
	147	T-17	-	16	19 pilots
Tel Nof	103	C-47	-	9	24 pilots, 7 copilots, 13 navigators,
		Noratlas	-	2	15 radio operators, 1 gunner
	115	Mosquito	1	1	4 pilots, 4 navigators
	116	P-51	14	2	16 pilots
	117	Meteor	12 (including one recce)	-	11 pilots
Hatzor	HQ	T-17	-	2	2 pilots
		T-6	-	3	
	101	Mystère	15 (including one recce)	14	19 pilots
	113	Ouragan	18	1	16 pilots
Beer Sheba	100C	Piper	not reported	not reported	not reported
Teman Field	140	T-6	16	-	25 pilots
Eilat	100D	Piper	1	-	not reported

Day 2
30 OCTOBER 1956

The ILAF's main objective for Day 2 was to accomplish a link-up between Brigade 202 and Battalion 890. ILDF/G/Operations ordered AIR3 – on 29 October at 2245 – to prepare support for Brigade 202's assault on Nekhel during the morning of Day 2, but then a prior directive – to avoid ILAF offensive operations for as long as the EGAF would not initiate offensive operations – prevailed and at 2355 ILDF/G/Operations notified Brigade 202 that there would be no ILAF support for the attack against Nekhel.

FROM MIDNIGHT TO SUNRISE

103	FAQ	Ofer/Shamir/ Zioni/Nimrod	drop Mitle
103	FAR	Thor/Kohen	drop Mitle
203	Noratlas	French/Goldreich	drop Mitle

While Squadron 103 and Squadron 203 flew Night 1 second wave missions to supply Battalion 890 at Mitle, AIR3 started to issue MIORs for Day 2.

MIOR Yud142, issued at 0035, tasked Squadron 101 to patrol along the route from Quntila to Mitle in order to defend Brigade 202 and Battalion 890. Four pairs were to take-off from 0545 until 0630 at 15-minute intervals. The fifth and sixth pairs were scheduled to take-off at 0700 and 0730. Pairs were to fly to and from the patrol sector at 35,000 feet. Over the patrol sector, pairs were to fly at 10,000 feet for

Squadron 200 - an ILAF shadow designation for FRAF F-84F unit - arrived at Lod on 30 October 1956; the FRAF F-84Fs were painted with ILAF badges and with ILAF Suez War IFF stripes version 1.

Squadron 201 Mystère taxiing at Ramat David. The two FRAF Mystère squadrons deployed to Israel - ILAF shadow Squadron 199 with ILAF aircraft and ILAF shadow Squadron 201 with FRAF aircraft – were specifically to bridge the gap between Israel's start of hostilities and the Anglo-French launch of air superiority offensive in order to defend Israel from EGAF Il-28 bombers during daytime, during the timeframe when ILAF would not have air superiority.

15 minutes while in radio contact with Battalion 890 FAC – radio call sign GIFT – and Brigade 202, which had two attached FAC Mobiles, call signs NIGHTINGALE and HEDGEHOG. Mysteres were to be armed with rocket pods but MIOR emphasized:

> Under no circumstances [are aircraft authorized] to open fire at [enemy] ground forces even if asked for by [ILDF] units in the field. Aircraft will be fired at only if these [enemy aircraft] will attack [ILDF] ground forces or our aircraft.

MIOR Yud143, issued at 0130, ordered Squadron 101 to dispatch two Mysteres at 0615 to recce routes from Bir Gafgafa to Bir Hama, Abu Ageila, El Arish and Rafah in order to evaluate EGDF deployment. The aircraft were to cruise from base to recce route at 37,000 feet and fly over the route at optimal altitude for visual recce. The MIOR was to be repeated from 1630.

MIOR Yud155, issued at 0150, tasked Squadron 101 to dispatch two Mysteres at 0615 for recce from Mitle to the Suez Canal and then north, along the Suez Canal, over the east bank and up to Ismailia. Pilots were to fly at optimal altitude for recce but were forbidden from crossing the canal and flying over the west bank.

Both MIOR Yud143 and Yud155 were canceled at 0505.

PLAN FOR SEAB EGYPT

Anglo-French forces were planned to initiate a SEAB offensive against the EGAF during the night of 30 to 31 October in order to win air superiority. Israel prepared for a worst-case scenario – in case Anglo-French forces would not attack Egypt – and the ILAF planned an optional Day 2 SEAB offensive against the EGAF with AIR3 issuing a series of MIORs, Yud144 to Yud154.

MIOR Yud144, issued at 0235, tasked Squadron 101 to launch three four-ship formations to SEAB Cairo West – with Almaza as a secondary target – with TOT at H-Hour, H plus 10 minutes and H plus 20 minutes. Six Mysteres were to be armed with rockets pods and six Mysteres with rockets pods plus belly rockets. Pilots would fly to the target at 35,000 feet, attack aircraft and hangars, and RTB at 35,000 feet. MIOR Yud145 tasked Squadron 101 to attack Kabrit – with Kasfareet as its secondary target – with six Mysteres, each armed with rockets pods.

MIOR Yud146 tasked Squadron 117 to raid Cairo West in two waves of six and four Meteors, with TOT at H plus 30 minutes and H plus 40 minutes. The Meteors were to fly to the target at 30,000 feet, strafe aircraft and hangars and RTB at 30,000 feet.

MIOR Yud150 tasked Squadron 116 to SEAB Kabrit – with Kasfareet as a secondary target – with eight P-51s at H plus 15 minutes and four P-51s at H plus 20 minutes. The P-51s were to be armed with two cluster bombs each, attack aircraft and hangars and fly to and from target at low altitude. AIR3 ordered squadrons to prepare for MIOR Yud144 to Yud154 from sunrise, but the ILAF SEAB offensive was not launched and the ILAF would operate over Sinai for two full days without prior accomplishment of air superiority, since the start of the Anglo-French SEAB offensive would be delayed from the evening of Day 2 to the evening of Day 3.

PIPERS TO MITLE

−0315	100	0443	Kadmon
			Eilat–JAMAICA, first landing at
			JAMAICA
0515–	100	0443	Kadmon JAMAICA
0515–	100	0444	Lolav/Brigade202scout
			somewhere in Sinai
0515–	100	0447	Bokai
			Beer Sheba–JAMAICA

Brigade 202 Flight Pipers, dispatched from Eilat during the evening of Day 1, did not land at JAMAICA because a landing strip

Piper 43 probably suffered light damage during take-off accident at Mitle on 30 October 1956 at 0515 but was then damaged again, this time so seriously that it was classed as CAT4, during extrication from Mitle by S-55 helicopter.

was not prepared. At 0230, Brigade 202 requested CASEVAC from ILDF/G/Operations, presumably on behalf of Battalion 890. The pace of advance of Brigade 202 – especially in light of the expected absence of air superiority over Sinai during Day 2 – worried the ILDF so, at 0320, ILDF/G/Operations ordered Command South to prepare a battalion from Brigade 8 for landing at Mitle in case Brigade 202 and Battalion 890's link-up would not be accomplished on time. At about that time, Squadron 100 was tasked to deliver a radio code book from Command South to Battalion 890; Moshe Bokai was assigned to recce the route from Quntila to Mitle and deliver the radio code book in 0456, but at 0445, while taxiing at Beer Sheba – in blackout, darkness and fog – Piper 56 collided with 0445 and both aircraft suffered CAT2 damage. Bokai switched to 0447, in which Brigade 202 Flight pilot Moshe Even returned from Lod, and pressed ahead with his mission.

At about the same time that Bokai departed Beer Sheba, Brigade 202 Flight pilot Zvi Kadmon, accompanied by a Battalion 890 scout, took off from JAMAICA in order to search for supply packages that were dropped during the night, but the Piper stalled during take-off and crashed; the pilot and passenger were unhurt.

Also at that time, Amnon Lolav took off from somewhere in Sinai and attempted to land beside Division 38 forces; the landing was harsh and Piper 44 suffered CAT2 damage.

DEFENSIVE PATROLS

0545–0648	101white1	4533	Shapira	
	Yud142 patrol Mitle			
0545–0648	101white2	4529	Harel	ditto
0600–0705	101brown1	4562	Morgan	
	Yud142 patrol Mitle			
0600–0705 ditto	101brown2	4592	Golan	
0600–	117	Meteor	Yoeli	patrol Sinai
0600–	117	Meteor	Sapir	ditto
0600–	117	Meteor	Altman	ditto
0600–	117	Meteor	Gat	ditto
0615–0710	101green1	4593	Bar	
	Yud142 patrol Mitle			

Squadron 101 log indicated that both Shlomo Bet-On and Dror Avneri flew Mystère 43 as green 2 and black 2, respectively, from 0615 and 0620, respectively, on 30 October 1956, but this was obviously impossible and was most likely a typo. This photo was taken after 0600 on 2 November 1956 as 4543 is marked with ILAF Suez War IFF stripes version 2. Pilots in front of 4543, from left to right: Jacob Gur, Uri Dekel and Dan Gonen.

0615–0710	101green2	4543)	BetOn	ditto
0620–0730	101yellow1	4546	Alon	
	Yud142 patrol Mitle			
0620–0730	101yellow2	4595	Shadmi	ditto
0620–0750	101black1	4543	Avneri	
	Yud142 patrol Mitle			
0620–0750	101black2	4549	Gilboa	ditto
0648–0745	101purple1	4552	Gonen	
	Yud142 patrol Mitle			
0648–0745	101purple2	4561	Gur	ditto

Squadron 199 and 201 patrolled over Israel while Squadron 101 patrolled over Sinai. Squadron 101 pilots reported movements of Egyptian forces from the Suez Canal in the direction of Mitle, presumably to attack Battalion 890, so the ILDF reported, at 0610, a Brigade 202 request for air support. In line with the ILDF directive and MIOR Yud142 guidelines, the Mysteres did not attack.

Brigade 202 occupied Thamad at 0640 and Brigade 4 occupied Quseima at 0700. Squadron 117 Meteor pilots reported that Bir Gafgafa and Bir Hama airfields were empty of enemy aircraft, while a significant EGDF deployment was noted at Abu Ageila.

EGAF ATTACK

	115	2139	Tavor	test
	140	1153	Gideoni/Vronski	
		Beer Sheba–Tel Nof–BeerSheba		
circa 0900	100	Piper	Hirsh	
		CASEVAC Thamad		
circa 0900	100	Piper	Cooperman	ditto
circa 0900	100	Piper	Greenbaum	ditto
circa 0900	100	Piper	Hasson	ditto
circa 0900	100	Piper	Wolf	ditto

MIOR Yud142 ordered Squadron 101 to launch six Mystère pairs for patrol over Mitle from 0545 until 0730 in order to accomplish continuous coverage from circa 0600 until circa 0815. Squadron 101 launched six pairs but these took off from 0545 until 0648 for actual coverage from circa 0600 until circa 0730. Since AIR3 did not issue MIOR to continue to patrol over Mitle, and as Squadron 101's sixth pair took off at 0648, there were no ILAF patrols over Sinai from 0730 until 0930. It was then that EGAF aircraft appeared over Mitle.

At first, EGAF Vampires flew over Battalion 890 but did not attack. Then, circa 0800, MiG-15s attacked Battalion 890. Moshe Bokai reported:

> My mission was to recce road from Quntila to Mitle and to deliver radio codes book to Battalion 890; my aircraft was equipped with stretcher and Mark 300 radio. I landed beside our forces, delivered radio codes book to [Battalion 890 Commander Rafael] Raful [Eitan] and he tasked me to evacuate to Beer Sheba an injured paratrooper with a broken leg. The injured paratrooper was inserted into the aircraft and I was ready to take-off but when I wanted to start engine, I sensed shooting, fuel spilled on me and the aircraft caught fire. I jumped out, extinguished my burning clothes [returned to the burning aircraft] and extracted the wounded [man] through the window. The aircraft was completely burnt out.

Four troops – including Bokai and Battalion 890's Medical Officer – were injured. MiG-15s then attacked Brigade 202 at Thamad circa 0815 and again at 0900; three troops were injured during the second strike, so Squadron 100 Pipers flew CASEVAC.

PHOTOGRAPH SINAI

0905–1000	117	Meteor	Lavon	
		Yud156 photograph Sinai		
0905–	117	3609	Zivoni	escort	Yud156
0905–1005	117	3734	Sarig	ditto

ILDF/I's requirement was delivered to the ILAF at 0030; AIR3 issued MIOR Yud156 at 0405. Squadron 117 flew the low altitude mission and the negatives were handed over to Squadron 115's laboratory at 1030; the laboratory processed 112 frames and produced 336 prints by 1255, the first interpretation report was issued at 1145 and prints were posted to addressees from 1220.

PATROL SINAI

0925–1045	101white1	4593	Bar
	Yud142 patrol Sinai		

EGAF MiG-15s attacked and destroyed Squadron 100 Piper 47 at Mitle, at about 0800 on 30 October 1956. Pilot Moshe Bokai was injured but regardless of injury successfully extricated a wounded trooper trapped in the burning Piper.

Squadron 101 pilot Ohad Shadmi flew MIOR Yud142 in Mystère 90 as black 2 on the morning of 30 October 1956.

0925–1045	101white2	4563	BetOn	ditto
1010–1125	101black1	4584	Alon	
	Yud142 patrol Sinai			
1010–1125	101black2	4590	Shadmi	ditto
1020–1135	101red1	4530	Morgan	
	Yud142 patrol Sinai			
1020–1135	101red2	4585	Golan	ditto
1055–1145	101green1	4543	Peled	
	Yud142 patrol Sinai			
1055–1145	101green2	4549	Ronen	ditto

In the wake of EGAF attacks, AIR3 ordered Squadron 101, at 0845, to renew Yud142 patrols with take-offs at 0915, 0945, 1015, 1045, 1115 and 1145.

The ILDF reported, at 0920, a Brigade 202 request for air support in a planned attack against Nekhel. As indicated, ILDF/G/Operations ordered Command South to prepare a battalion from Brigade 8 for landing at Mitle in case the Brigade 202 and Battalion 890 link-up was not accomplished on time. Squadron 103 reported, at 0950, the arrival of the Battalion 92 Deputy Commander for the coordination of planned flights to Mitle.

MiG-15s attacked Battalion 890 at 0955; by then, Squadron 101 white section was patrolling over Sinai but no air combat ensued. Squadron 101 white section pilots reported observing Brigade 202 forces advancing from Thamad to Nekhel and rejected a request

Reportedly the wreckage of Piper 32 in which Squadron 100 Eilat HQ pilot Benjamin Kahane and ILDF/I Eilat HQ scout David Cohen were killed on 30 October 1956.

from Battalion 890 to attack Egyptian forces that targeted ILDF paratroopers with mortars.

Finally, the ILAF was authorized to attack Egyptian forces west of Battalion 890. First to open fire was Squadron 101 black section, with red and green sections following.

PIPER VERSUS MIG-15

100   0432   Kahane/Cohen

Squadron 100 originally deployed nine Pipers to Eilat; eight were allocated to Flight D, which initially supported Brigade 202, and one was assigned to Eilat HQ. While flying an Eilat HQ mission, Eilat HQ pilot Benjamin Kahane encountered enemy aircraft. The only report thus far unearthed concerning enemy aircraft operations over the Eilat sector during Day 2 is an AIR4 report from 1700 on 30 October:

> MiG aircraft attacked cars convoy on its way to Eilat; a number of casualties had been inflicted.

It is not known, at the time of writing, if the MiGs that attacked vehicles on the way to Eilat were the same MiGs that the Eilat HQ Piper encountered. Runway Unit 666 – operating Eilat airfield – reported at 1900:

> Patrol that searched for 0432 reported a crashed and burnt-out Piper aircraft at map reference 124933. Tomorrow, at first light, a ground patrol... will depart [Eilat] to [crash] site...

Squadron 100 Flight D Commander Isaac Hirsh reported the following day:

> Captain Kahane was attacked yesterday, before noon, east of Quntila, and was shot down. An Eilat HQ scout was in the aircraft. Cooperman searched for him, pinpointed [wreckage] and reported that from the air it looks like both occupants were killed. Today, a ground force departed [from Eilat] to [crash] site and did not return yet.

Eilat HQ Commander (Acting) Uri Shilo reported on 11 November:

During the night of 29 to 30 October 1956, during attack against Ras Naqab police station, Eilat HQ scout unit was tasked to block Ras Naqab–Thamad route, some 12 kilometers deep [inside Sinai] but communication with [Eilat HQ scout] unit did not function and Captain Benjamin Kahane acted as relay with the scout unit.

At 0400, after the police station had been occupied, Command South ordered [Eilat HQ] to take over Quntila police station. Radio of tasked unit did not function so the aircraft, along with an intelligence sergeant, was dispatched, circa 1000, to communicate with the unit.

According to testimonies of eyewitnesses whom I am unable to name (they passed through Quntila and continued west) it turned out that two MiGs attacked the Piper some five kilometers south of Quntila. Captain Kahane engaged them in evasion combat for some 15 minutes until one of the MiGs hit him and he fell.

I recommend award of a citation to Captain Benjamin Kahane for the evasion combat that he fought versus two MiG aircraft.

OURAGANS JOIN MYSTERES

1105–1205	101blue1	4562	Nevo	patrol Sinai
1105–1205	101blue2	4592	Zuk	ditto
1155–1255	100	Piper	Harpaz/ scout	Ktziot–Ktziot
1200–	113	Ouragan	Hod	patrol Sinai
1200–1315	113	4052	Sheffer	ditto
1215–1335	101 silver1	4529	Egozi	patrol Sinai
1215–1335	101 silver2	4561	Shavit	ditto
1215–	113	Ouragan	Sharon	patrol Sinai
1215–	113	Ouragan	Rosen	ditto
1230–1340	101red1	4533	Shapira	patrol Sinai
1230–1340	101red2	4545	Harel	ditto

EGAF aircraft continued to attack Mitle regardless of Mystère presence. The ILDF indicated, at 1100, a Brigade 202 FAC Mobile Number 24 report that two MiGs attacked Mitle while, at the same time, Command South reported to ILDF that enemy aircraft attacked Brigade 202, which suffered several casualties; the ILDF indicated again, at 1120, another Brigade 202 report concerning enemy aircraft attack. Due to normal delay in reporting, the attacks probably took place sometime before 1100 and 1120.

ILAF pre-war doctrine was accomplishment of air superiority prior to air support, but politics precluded an ILAF air superiority campaign so the ILAF had to wait for the Anglo-French air superiority offensive. For the meantime, the ILAF restrained from tasking Mosquitoes and P-51s to fly air support missions and initially dispatched to Mitle only Squadron 101 Mysteres because all other ILAF jet types were inferior to MiG-15. ILAF policy was slightly relaxed from 1200 when the first Squadron 113 Ouragan pair – tasked to patrol over Mitle and to attack enemy forces – departed Hatzor.

Squadron 101 Mysteres and Squadron 113 Ouragans operated over Sinai, east of the Suez Canal, and mostly attacked along the road from Suez to Mitle, but at 1215 the ILDF noted that Shalufa – west of the Suez Canal – was attacked; it is not yet known which aircraft attacked Shalufa.

Ten minutes later, at 1225, the ILDF approved a Brigade 202 request for air support in a planned attack against Nekhel.

SIGHTINGS OF ENEMY AIRCRAFT

1230–1340	101red1	4533	Shapira	patrol Sinai
1230–1340	101red2	4545	Harel	ditto
1305–1410	113	4043	Agassi	support Btn 890
1305–1410	113	Ouragan	Erez	ditto
1305–1410	113	4061	Kishon	ditto
1305–1410	113	4062	Ivry	ditto
1320–1445	115	3517	Livneh/Sivron	
		Yud135 photograph Sinai		
1320–1440	117	3733	Kaspit	
		Yud136 escort Yud135		
1320–1420	117	3734	Yahalom	ditto

Squadron 101 red section attacked Egyptian forces west of Mitle and reported the sighting of a MiG-15, but no air combat ensued. The Ouragans did not attack. MIOR Yud136 tasked Squadron 115 to photograph the Division 38 sector of operations, including Bir Hama and Jabel Libni, before the launch of the offensive, from high altitude with 36in camera. Two MiG-15s were sighted over Bir Hama but again no air combat ensued; the mission produced 205 negatives and 615 prints that were posted from 1835.

CABLE CUT AGAIN

1325–	116	2329	Zeelon	cable cutter
1325–1555	116	2306	Fredilis	ditto
1325–	116	P-51	Hasson	cable cut
1325–	116	P-51	Naveh	ditto
1340–	113	Ouragan	Harlev	support Btn 890
1340–	113	Ouragan	Furman	ditto
1340–	113	Ouragan	Halivni	ditto
1340–	113	Ouragan	Zahavi	ditto
1345–1445	117	Meteor		support
1345–1445	117	Meteor		ditto
1345–1445	117	Meteor		ditto
1345–1445	117	Meteor		ditto

Squadron 103 was ordered, at 1330, to place two C-47s on alert for CASEVAC from Mitle, but airlifters were not yet allowed to fly over Sinai during daylight. Half an hour later, at 1400, the ILDF ordered Command South to stop Division 38's attack on Abu Ageila while Brigade 7 was ordered to plan a morning attack with air support. Squadron 117 Meteors probably attacked a convoy nearby Khan Yunes and claimed the destruction of six vehicles.

SCRAMBLE TO KABRIT

1415–	113	Ouragan	Dan	support Btn 890
1415–	113	Ouragan	Ayalon	ditto
1435–1550	101blue1	4563	Nevo	scramble to Mitle Kabrit
1435–1550	101blue	4593	Zuk	ditto
1435–1550	101blue	Mystère	Egozi	ditto
1435–1545	113	4049	Sheffer	support Btn 890
1435–1545	113	Ouragan	Yariv	ditto
1440–1550	101red1	Mystère	Shapira	support Btn 890

Squadron 101 pilot Josef Zuk standing beside the damaged wing of his Mystère 93 after air combat over Kabrit on 30 October 1956.

Close-up view of damage to the left wing of Mystère 93 during air combat over Kabrit on 30 October 1956.

1440–1550	101red2	Mystère	Shavit	ditto
1440–1540	101 yellow1	Mystère	Gonen	scramble to Mitle Kabrit
1440–1540	101 yellow	4564	Gilboa	ditto
1440–1540	101 yellow	Mystère	Avneri	ditto
1445–1600	101 khaki1	4584	Lev	scramble to Mitle Kabrit
1445–1600	101 khaki2	4590	Lapidot	ditto

ILDF/I intercepted, sometime before 1435, a radio message from EGDF Brigade 2 at Shalufa to EGDF Battalion 6 which, at that time, exchanged fire with ILDF Battalion 890:

> Four Egyptian aircraft are over you. Are there enemy aircraft around? Did Egyptian aircraft engage enemy aircraft? Our aircraft are over you.

This message was erroneously translated to read 24 aircraft. The error was corrected within a short while but, in the meantime, Squadron 101 Mysteres were scrambled to face 24 MiGs over the Mitle to Kabrit sector.

Squadron 101 blue section attacked four MiGs immediately after take-off from Kabrit and during this first pass, Josef Zuk hit a MiG that reportedly crashed. More MiGs – the ILAF narrative mentioned 12 MiGs – joined the combat and during the ensuing engagement Dror Avneri and Amos Lapidot reported hitting MiGs. Dror Avneri noted:

Two MiGs were shot down [and] one was [MiG was] probably shot down; I was credited with one of the shot downs.

The ILDF noted, at 1545, an initial AIR3 report:

Two to three MiGs were shot down over Kabrit. Two [Mystère] aircraft are short of fuel; one [Mystère] fell into sea near El Arish.

The AIR3 initial report was erroneous, as all Squadron 101 Mysteres RTBed. At 1705, AIR4 reported:

MiG aircraft was shot down over Kabrit air base and a second [MiG] was destroyed during take-off from field (confirmation required).

Post-war, the ILAF acknowledged one kill over Kabrit during this first Mystère versus MiG-15 engagement and Squadron 101 Mystère pilot Josef Zuk was credited with a kill.

Meanwhile, Squadron 101 red section attacked west of Mitle and claimed the destruction of four vehicles out of a column of 16 vehicles seen to advance in the direction of Battalion 890.

ILDF ORDERS FOR DAY 3

1523–1620	101 green1	Mystère	Peled	patrol Sinai
1523–1620	101 green2	Mystère	Ronen	ditto
1530	113	4041	Agassi	support Btn 890
1530	113	Ouragan	Bareket	ditto
1530–1620	101 black1	4535	Alon	patrol Sinai
1530–1620	101 black2	4535	Shadmi	ditto
1605	113	Ouragan	Sharon	support Btn 890
1605	113	Ouragan	Rosen	ditto
1605	113	Ouragan	Halivni	support Btn 890
1605	113	Ouragan	Furman	ditto
1605	113	4047	Kishon	support Btn 890
1605	113	Ouragan	Erez	ditto, abort, RTB

The ILDF issued to Command South, at 1500, orders for Day 3:

– Brigade 7 tasked to occupy Bir Hasana and if possible then Abu Ageila and Jabel Libni as well.
– Brigade 4 tasked to replace Brigade 202.
– Brigade 9 tasked to start advance in direction of Sharm El Sheikh.

Ouragan pilots claimed the destruction of four trucks, a tracked vehicle and one gun in napalm, rocketry and gunnery attacks. At 1700, AIR4 reported that an EGDF attack against Battalion 890 had been repelled.

INTERDICTION WEST OF MITLE

1608–	117	Meteor	Yoeli	support Btn 890
1608–	117	Meteor	Sapir	ditto
1608–	117	Meteor	Altman	ditto
1608–	117	Meteor	Gat	ditto

1610–1715	101	Mystère	Bar white1	patrol Sinai
1610–1715	101	Mystère	Morgan white2	ditto

Tel Nof reported the departure of four Meteors at 1608, while debrief take-off time entry was 1620; either way, Meteor pilots strafed Egyptian forces west of Battalion 890 and claimed the destruction of several vehicles.

ILAF support to Battalion 890 was rated successful. Most pilots attacked EGDF vehicles and troops west of Battalion 890 and probably disrupted EGDF plans to attack Battalion 890; AIR4 reported – at 0045 on 31 October – that pilots supporting Battalion 890 claimed the destruction of some 40 trucks, six half-tracks and four tankers.

SUPPLIES TO MITLE AND NEKHEL

103	1416	Biran/Vossman Yud166 drop Nekhel	
103	1418	Rom/Ohad	drop Mitle
103	1432	Oz/Biran Yud165 drop Mitle, abort, RTB after ten minutes in the air	
103	C-47	psywar Abu Ageila	
103	FAQ	BenJosef/ Bliman/Levanon/Kobo	drop Mitle

Brigade 202 reportedly attacked Nekhel at 1700 and occupied Nekhel by 1720. The ILDF noted Brigade 202 reports slightly later: occupation of Nekhel was reported at 1815 and advance from Nekhel to Mitle was reported at 1900.

Meanwhile, at 1645, AIR3 tasked Squadron 103 to dispatch 17 C-47s for a drop of supplies to Brigade 202 during the night of 30 to 31 October. Sometime later, Squadron 103 reported the availability – on top of two C-47s on readiness for CASEVAC, one C-47 on readiness with flares for illumination and one C-47 with loudspeakers for psywar (psychological warfare) – of nine aircraft and nine crews, as well as the intention to fly missions in singles, in trail.

Runway Unit 625 was attached to Brigade 202 and the plan was to open a runway nearby the Battalion 890 drop zone after the link-up between Brigade 202 and Battalion 890. However, the link-up was not accomplished at the time of the first wave, from sunset to midnight, so the original plan for an airlift had to be changed to an air drop as, at 1845, Tel Nof indicated:

Airlift will not be operated tonight because a landing field at JAMAICA had not been prepared; the aircraft will drop the supplies.

Both Battalion 890 and Brigade 202 suffered casualties. At 2020, Tel Nof reported:

Two C-47s departed to JAMAICA for CASEVAC in the hope that the field would be ready for landing; the aircraft orbited overhead but field was not prepared and aircraft RTBed.

In addition to the airlift and CASEVAC, Squadron 103 was also tasked to fly psywar mission over Abu Ageila with an aircraft equipped with loudspeakers. At 2215, Squadron 103 reported:

FRAF Mysteres flew daylight defensive patrols to protect Israel from EGAF Il-28 bombings, thus freeing Squadron 101 to operate over Sinai, but EGAF Il-28s did not operate during daylight during the Suez War. These Squadron 199 Mysteres were actually ILAF aircraft flown by French pilots.

ILAF fielded three Meteor night fighters and one crew to counter EGAF Il-28 nighttime bombings threat. There are no known photos of ILAF Meteor night fighters from the time of the Suez War; this photo of 3852 was taken on 14 January 1957.

> [AIR3 ordered] to dispatch the aircraft with loudspeakers, immediately and without an additional briefing; the aircraft departed.

INTERDICTION SINAI

2240–	110	Mosquito	Somech interdiction Sinai

The first Suez War offensive Mosquito mission was to bomb Egyptian forces along the route from Port Taufik to Mitle. The Mosquito crew was unable to pinpoint the road from Port Taufik to Mitle so flew north, observed traffic, with lights on, along the road from Ismailia to Bir Gafgafa and bombed there.

EGYPTIAN BOMBINGS

	119	3852	Tsiddon/Brosh	
				patrol Sinai
	119	3852	Tsiddon/Brosh	scramble

Israel expected an EGAF Il-28 offensive, so Squadron 199 and Squadron 201 flew patrols during daylight – AIR3 issued, at 1950, MIOR Yud168 that tasked Squadron 199 to launch two four-ship formations, at 0530 and 0630, on 31 October, to patrol over Ashkelon at 37,000 feet, with Squadron 200 F-84s patrolling at 15,000 feet, while Squadron 119 was on readiness during nighttime.

EGAF Il-28s indeed attacked Israel during the evening. The first thus far unearthed report concerning a possible Il-28 attack is from 2100, when Command South reported to the ILDF an air raid. AIR4 subsequently reported the next known events:

> At 2150 an enemy jet aircraft appeared over Tel Aviv, probably with intention to bomb [Tel Aviv] but the bombs fell into the sea opposite Bat Yam coast. A second enemy jet aircraft bombed, without success, at 2215, nearby Ramat Raziel, a train travelling to Jerusalem with lights on.

It was at 2350 that Command Center reported to the ILDF:

> A jet aircraft bombed railway nearby Ramat Raziel at 2215. Train travelling to Jerusalem stopped. More details to follow.

More details followed at 0010 when Command Center reported to the ILDF:

> A jet aircraft followed the train that departed Jerusalem, with lights on, in direction of Lod, and aimed a bomb at it nearby Ramat Raziel; train and railroad were not hit; several telephone lines were damaged.

A post-war MAT5 investigation added a few details:

> A resident of Ramat Raziel, who was on watch that night, told that he heard the sound of an approaching aircraft and at the same time he saw a train travelling with lights on. Immediately afterwards he heard a loud explosion. Along with two Ramat Raziel residents, we looked for hits. We scanned area along railway but were unable to pinpoint location of hits. Public works workers who worked nearby, building a road, told us that an engineer from public works department in Jerusalem knows the location of the hits and has a collection of fragments.

AIR4, on 28 December, summed up the ILAF perspective of EGAF Il-28 operations during the night of 30 to 31 October:

> Bombs were dropped nearby Ramat Raziel; remains of bomb tails were examined and the bombs were identified as Russian. Several FACs reported bombings in sectors of Abu Ageila, Ktziot and Quntila; it was impossible to retrieve parts of bombs for identification. Central Control Unit reported tracks of enemy aircraft over Sinai and especially over Mitle, over south Israel and west of Haifa. Intercepted radio communications almost certainly confirm that Il-28 aircraft were in the air. In some cases there was correlation in data from radar tracks and from radio intercepts.

The Squadron 119 Meteor crew did not make contact with Il-28s and in any case no damage was caused, as all bombs fell and exploded in open ground.

DIVISION 77 AIR SUPPORT REQUEST

Brigade 202 reportedly linked-up with Battalion 890 at 2300; the ILDF noted Brigade 202's link-up report at 2359. Around that time, the first wave of Squadron 103's drop of supplies to Brigade 202 and Battalion 890 had ended, while at about the same time, at 2345, Division 77 ALO Leslie David Easterman requested planned air support:

Division 77 is about to attack Rafah and to advance for occupation of El Arish. Proposition for support plan is divided for support at night and support during daylight.

At night. Rafah camps... traffic between Rafah and El Arish. El Arish railway station...

During daylight. Precision attacks... First priority all types of armored vehicles... traffic along route Rafah–El Arish. Interdiction... Second priority: artillery and mortars at map reference... Third priority: camp at... fortifications at... Fourth priority: light AAA at... Absolute priority for attack of armor...

Day 3
31 OCTOBER 1956

ILDF plans for Day 3 were to continue Division 38's attack in the center sector, initiate Division 77's offensive in the north sector and continue Brigade 9's advance in the direction of Sharm El Sheikh.

NIGHT INTRUDERS

	110	2169	Ash/ Segal	interdiction Sinai
	110	2177	Shemer	interdiction Sinai
0320 –0530	110	2167	Levy/ Proshanski	interdiction Sinai

Mosquito crews were tasked to target traffic along roads in Sinai, operating in singles, at progressive timeframes. Ash/Segal attacked traffic along RADISH and SPINACH; Shemer operated over the El Arish sector; Proshanski/Levy attacked along RADISH and returned on one engine for a successful SEL.

IBRAHIM EL AWAL ATTACK

04:45–0730	103	1404	Kohen/Richter/Levanon/ scramble to support ILNF	Cohen

Haifa port was bombarded from 0340 until 0350. AIR3 was notified at 0410 so AIR3 duty officer David Yaeli ordered to scramble illumination readiness C-47 – an aircraft that was equipped with APS-4 radar – and to change the readiness timeframe of four Squadron 116 P-51s from one hour to immediate take-off after scramble order.

Prior to bombardment, at 0245, the ILNF radar station pinpointed

Some Squadron 103 C-47s were equipped with AN/APS-4 radar, primarily for maritime patrol. This aircraft was photographed during the Suez War; crouching fifth from left is almost certainly Israel Ben-Shahar, Division 38 ALO during the Suez War.

two unidentified targets west of Haifa lighthouse at 20 miles' range; the targets were heading east at 20 knots. By 0315, ILNF radar operators concluded that the two targets were actually one target, still unidentified. In the wake of bombardment, an ILNF officer arrived at ILAF Control Unit 503, on top of Mount Carmel in Haifa, in order to track the enemy warship that bombarded Haifa port. Cooperation between the ILAF and ILNF radar operators yielded a track and at 0432 the ILNF reported to Flotilla 1, tasked to intercept enemy warships, that the enemy was at 300 degrees from Haifa lighthouse, at a range of 15 miles and at 25 knots.

Meanwhile, French destroyer Kersaint, on AAA readiness in Haifa bay, identified the EGNF ship and fired 64 shells – reportedly optimized for AAA and not for penetration of warship armor – but was unable to pursue due to a malfunction that limited speed to 15 knots.

ILNF Flotilla 1 destroyers detected the EGNF warship at 0507 and opened fire at 0532. An ILNF request for air support was issued at 0510 and included the enemy position – as pinpointed at 0505 – at 310 degrees from Haifa lighthouse, at a range of 31 miles and at 25 knots. Three minutes later, at 0513, Tel Nof reported that Squadron 116 pilots – four P-51s were on readiness to attack the ship with napalm and rockets – were briefed how to attack the enemy ship.

The C-47 arrived over the scene at 0515; morning had broken – though actual sunrise was at 0555 – and there was no need for illumination, but the C-47 continued to shadow the enemy warship. Gideon Kohen recalled:

> I was on duty in the squadron and slept on top of the parachutes closet when I was woken up and we were scrambled in an aircraft with flares. We received heading and distance from Mount Carmel; along our way to the spot, where the ship was supposed to be, it was still dark and we pinpointed tracks of unidentified ships but we flew on until we arrived over the spot where the ship was supposed to be, but it was not there so I told navigator Johanan Levanon that we would start square search. We started square search, by then morning had broken, and after a short while we saw three ships; one in front and two in pursuit. We contacted [Flotilla 1] and asked 'do you want help?'. They replied 'hold on' and then 'no' so we orbited overhead and then my co-pilot [Samuel] Richter asked my permission to contact [Flotilla 1] and I answered 'go ahead'; he asked [Flotilla 1] if they would like us to request attack aircraft and this time the reply was 'yes'.

ILDF/I intercepted radio messages between the ship and EGNF HQ and concluded that the ship in question was EGNF Ibrahim el Awal, Abraham the First, a destroyer.

COMBAT OVER MITLE

0530–0640	101silver1	4562	Egozi	Yud170 patrol Mitle
0530–0640	101silver2	4533	Shavit	ditto

EGDF units that advanced from the Suez Canal to Mitle, in order to attack Battalion 890, were by then in defensive deployment at Mitle Pass. The ILDF ordered Brigade 202, at 0500, not to attack Mitle Pass. Brigade 202 and Battalion 890 linked-up but postponement, for 24 hours, of the Anglo-French air superiority offensive exposed ILDF

Possibly wreckage of one of the EGAF Vampires shot down near Mitle on the morning of 31 October 1956.

Mystère 30 as photographed in June 1957 with one kill markings. Mystère 62 is not known to have been painted with kill markings; the pilot in the cockpit is Joel Dan, who flew Squadron 113 Ouragans during the Suez War.

units in Sinai to potential EGAF strikes for another day. Therefore, AIR3 issued, at 0235, MIOR Yud170 that tasked Squadron 101 to dispatch Mysteres, from 0545, to protect Brigade 202. The Mysteres were to be armed with full internal ammunition but no external ordnance, fly to Mitle at 30,000 feet and return from Mitle at 30,000 feet. MIOR Yud170 also stressed:

> Upon arrival over target, Number 1 will call the unit over [radio] channel B call sign GIFT. The aircraft will report to GIFT any enemy movement from [Suez] Canal in direction of our forces. Do not fly west of meridian 790 in Egyptian grid. Attack enemy east of meridian 790 [in Egyptian grid].

Circa 0600, GIFT reported to Squadron 101 silver section the presence of EGAF Vampires; AIR4 post-war air combats analysis stated:

> Three Vampires were shot down during an air combat that lasted for only one minute. The pilot [Shy Egozi] described:
> We already intended to RTB when GIFT reported sighting of four Vampires. We descended from 25,000 feet to 10,000 feet and then we saw them. They flew in close formation, in two pairs, aircraft in each pair were 20 yards apart and the pairs were 200 yards apart. During dive in direction of Vampires they turned 90 degrees, which eased getting into [efficient gunnery] range. I opened fire, one aircraft was hit and crashed. Three [Vampires] remained, one turned right and the pair turned left. My Number 2 followed the pair and shot down both in a single pass. The [enemy] aircraft did not drop external stores... during the engagement.
> Remarks:
> Close formation degraded flexibility during combat and enabled shooting down of two aircraft in a single attack (pass). Not jettisoning external stores during combat degraded maneuverability [of enemy aircraft].

AIR4 Intelligence Report Number 8, issued at 1130 on 31 October, summed up the engagement:

> Two Mysteres engaged a formation of six Vampires over drop zone. Three Vampires were shot down and it is possible that a fourth aircraft was hit and performed an emergency landing.

Reportedly - though this is not confirmed - Mystère 33 being painted with one-and-a-half kill markings in the wake of combat on 30 October 1956.

Mystère 33 with two full kill markings as photographed in May 1957.

Brigade 202 ALO Israel Lahav, in his post-war report, summed up:

> Four Vampires conducted an armed reconnaissance – three of them were shot down by a pair of Mysteres.

PXNE and AMV1 narratives acknowledged the loss of three Vampires, and AMV1 presented a quotation of Vampire pilot Talaat Louca:

> On that mission, Bahgat [Hassan Helmi] and his Number 2 [Mahmoud Wael Afifi] were shot down and killed. One pilot, named Ahmad Farghal, bailed out and the Number 4 got back safely.

IBRAHIM EL AWAL SURRENDER

0558–0655	113	4026	Agassi	scramble to support ILNF
0558–0655	113	4050	Kishon	ditto

Squadron 110 Mosquitoes – in addition to or instead of Squadron 116 P-51s – were also, reportedly, placed on alert to support the ILNF, or even ordered to scramble. Yet the aircraft that actually scrambled to support the ILNF were Ouragans that departed Hatzor 48 minutes after ILNF Flotilla 1 requested air support. Additionally, French Mysteres were scrambled from Ramat David after ILDF/I intercepted message from the EGNF to Ibrahim el Awal that Syrian aircraft would support the Egyptian warship. The Mysteres patrolled at high altitude but no Syrian aircraft appeared. Jacob Agassi recalled:

> I was on duty in the squadron when AIR3 telephoned and informed us that a ship had attacked Haifa and that we have to scramble two Ouragans to attack the ship. I ordered to arm the Ouragans with heavy T-10 rockets because it is very difficult to hit a slender ship with bombs so I decided to attack with rockets even though warships have dangerous AAA, but it was war!
> We flew over there and we did not find the ship. Control vectored us to sea opposite Atlit, again and again, and then opposite Haifa, again and again, and we did not see the ship even though weather was fine and visibility was good. Then [C-47 pilot] Gideon Kohen started to vector us and slowly, with vectors from Gideon Kohen who saw the ship, we detected the ship that was in fact opposite Acre. By then we were low on fuel so after I identified the ship, I attacked from east to west, along the length of the ship that was heading east, from very

> low altitude. I released all rockets in a single pass as I did not have enough fuel for a second pass; the rockets hit the ship, I saw the rockets streak into the ship, and as I broke away the ship emanated smoke or steam that covered the whole ship. Immediately afterwards we RTBed because we ran out of fuel; I thought that we would have to land at Ramat David but fuel sufficed for flight to Hatzor.

Presenting the same scene from a C-47 perspective, Gideon Kohen recalled:

> Control probably did not track aircraft and ships because Agassi searched for some time while we tried to guide him without success, and I heard Agassi saying to control 'find that ship ASAP because we are running out of fuel!'. At that time, communication was broken so I climbed. Control then tracked me and vectored Agassi in my direction. Agassi arrived and reported seeing ships so I told him 'it is the north-east ship' and he attacked immediately. A huge white cloud emanated from the ship, vertically, immediately after the attack. Then, sometime later, we were ordered to RTB and since, at some point, control warned us to beware of enemy aircraft, I RTBed at rooftop altitude. Normally we were not allowed to fly that low but I exploited the opportunity; my excuse was control warning concerning enemy aircraft.

ILNF ALO Pinchas Adler later remarked:

> The excellent cooperation between the lead C-47 and the attacking jets should be commended. The C-47 was glued to the target and although the Egyptian ship opened AAA fire, the C-47 did not move away. The attacking aircraft circled for a very long time over the enemy ship before they [positively] identified it [as an enemy ship] and it can be presumed that had the ship AAA been functioning properly then it could have shot down the attacking aircraft.

The Ouragans attacked at 0638, in a single run, due to low fuel as a result of the relatively long flight from Hatzor – ILNF ALO subsequently questioned why attack aircraft were not scrambled from the much-closer Ramat David – and the relatively long identification process. Each Ouragan launched 16 T-10 rockets and the lead Ouragan also strafed during the rocketry run.

Ibrahim el Awal stopped at 0700 and surrendered shortly afterwards.

Squadron 113 Deputy A Jacob Agassi flew Ouragan 26 to attack Ibrahim El Awal. Ouragan 26 was photographed while undergoing an undercarriage retraction maintenance; ILAF Suez War IFF stripes look like version 1.

Post-war investigation concluded that ILNF Flotilla 1 destroyers scored five hits out of 436 shells fired, ILAF Ouragans scored a single hit out of 32 rockets launched and the French destroyer did not hit Ibrahim el Awal.

METEORS VERSUS MIGS

Time	Squadron		Pilot	Mission
0620–0720	101 white1	4550	Bar	patrol Mitle
0620–0720	101 white2	4585	BetOn	ditto
0620–	117	Meteor	Ben Aaron	interdiction SPINACH
0620–	117	Meteor	Alroy	ditto
0634–	103	1401	Ofer/Peer/Zioni/Nimrod Tel Nof–Akrotiri–Tel Nof, VIP	

Squadron 101 white did not encounter enemy aircraft over Mitle so strafed Egyptian vehicles west of Brigade 202. At about the same time, Squadron 117 Meteors were tasked to strafe vehicles along SPINACH; over Jabel Libni, the two Meteors encountered four MiGs and the ensuing inconclusive combat lasted five minutes.

VAMPIRE DUMMIES AT EL ARISH

Time	Squadron		Pilot	Mission
0700–	113	Ouragan	Hod	scramble to support ILNF
0700–	113	Ouragan	Weizman	ditto
0710–0815	101 black1	4549	Alon	patrol Mitle
0710–0815	101 black2	4560	Shadmi	ditto

Squadron 113 Commander Moti Hod and Hatzor Wing 4 Commander Ezer Weizman were eager to take part in the maritime engagement between the EGNF and ILNF but were too late; they were retasked to attack traffic along RADISH, where an EGDF brigade was advancing from west to east, from the Suez Canal camps to the front line. Ouragan pilots claimed the destruction of seven vehicles, one gun and three artillery towing vehicles; they also reported sighting six Vampires at El Arish airfield; these were actually dummy Vampires and the EGAF is not known to have used El Arish at all during the Suez War.

An EGAF Vampire dummy at El Arish as photographed after ILDF occupation; pre-war AIR4 reports indicated that Sinai airfields were not in EGAF use and that EGAF Vampires were based at Suez Canal Zone airfields.

CASEVAC FROM EILAT

Time	Squadron	Type	Mission
0730–0850	103	C-47	Eilat–Tel Nof, CASEVAC

CASEVAC has always been an ILDF value but the Suez War's initial CASEVAC operations were somewhat sluggish. By the morning of Day 3, Squadron 100 Pipers evacuated 11 Brigade 202 casualties, but since each Piper could evacuate only one casualty at a time, and because a Piper's cruising speed was slower than the cruising speed of a C-47, this CASEVAC effort was slow and lasted overnight. An ILAF plan to utilize two C-47s for CASEVAC did not materialize because Brigade 202 did not prepare a field for landings of C-47s. Holding casualties in the field over a long timeframe was obviously undesirable so, at 0615, the ILDF noted an urgent request for CASEVAC from Command South:

> The Command [South] firmly requests to land a C-47 at Nekhel in order to evacuate casualties who were injured 12 hours ago.

At 0700, Command South reported that the field at Nekhel was ready but the ILAF restrained from tasking transport aircraft to fly during daytime until air superiority over Sinai had been secured. Daytime flights of ILAF airlifters during Day 2 and Day 3 – when the Anglo-French air superiority offensive had not yet been launched and as a result the EGAF operated over Sinai and the ILAF was not in possession of air superiority – were very restricted. The only thus far unearthed Squadron 103 CASEVAC mission, during Day 3 morning hours, was from Eilat to Tel Nof.

DIVISION 4 ARMOR BRIGADE 1

Time	Squadron		Pilot	Mission
0730–0825	117	3604	Kaspit Yud173	interdiction SPINACH
0730–0825	117	3606	Yahalom	ditto

The EGDF's main force – that the ILDF identified as Division 4 Armor Brigade 1 with an estimated strength of one T-34 tank battalion, one Sherman tank battalion, one Stalin tank company, one artillery battalion and support units – was advancing from the Suez Canal to the Sinai front line along SPINACH; the Meteors strafed in the sector of Jabel Libni, circa 0800, and claimed the destruction of two vehicles.

Reportedly an ILAF P-51 over ILDF troops during the Suez War - though it is possible that this image was not taken during the Suez War and was only captioned as such. Such a scene was only possible after 0745 on 31 October 1956 as ILAF P-51s did not fly Suez War attack missions prior to this time and date.

OCCUPATION ABU AGEILA

0745–	105	P-51	Tadmor	attack Abu Ageila
0745–1005	105	2310	Magen	ditto
0745–	105	P-51	Kopel	ditto
0745–1005	105	P-51	Zur	ditto

Brigade 7 was tasked to outflank the Om Kattef fortifications and to occupy Abu Ageila. In preparation for the attack, which was due to start at 0530, Brigade 7 FAC Asher Lavi requested air support including an attack on Egyptian fortifications in the Om Kattef to Abu Ageila sector and interdiction along roads from Abu Ageila to El Arish, from Abu Ageila to Bir Hasana and from Jabel Libni to Ismailia. Brigade 7's attack was successful and by 0700 Brigade 7 Battalion 82 occupied Abu Ageila.

The first P-51 formation tasked to fly an attack mission departed Ramat David at 0745 to attack Abu Ageila. However, exactly at 0745, the ILDF noted an 'Abu Ageila in our hands' report from Command South. On top of that, there was no FAC present at the Abu Ageila sector at that time – the Brigade 7 FAC was forced to return to Quseima due to mechanical problems with the FAC vehicle and the Brigade 10 FAC was east of Om Kattef – while many ILDF vehicles had not been properly marked to ease IFF due to short notice and shortage in paints; in any case, even when properly marked, it was very difficult to see from the air IFF marks painted on ILDF vehicles as desert dust covered all vehicles and in many cases practically concealed the properly-painted IFF marks.

The Squadron 105 formation was therefore retasked to attack enemy forces, mostly vehicles, in the Jabel Libni sector, some 40 kilometers west of Abu Ageila. There, the P-51s pinpointed a column of some 30 vehicles and claimed the destruction of ten vehicles, including two tracked vehicle and one tanker.

ATTACK EL ARISH

0745–	113	Ouragan	Halivni	scramble to support ILNF
0745–0815	113	4044	Ivry	ditto

Ibrahim el Awal had already surrendered by the time Amnon Halivni and David Ivry departed Hatzor, so the pair was retasked to raid El Arish airfield, where Moti Hod and Ezer Weizman had observed Vampires. Halivni and Ivry claimed the destruction of six Vampires – these were indeed dummies – as well as three light planes and several vehicles within the air base perimeter.

FIRST P-51 LOSS

0800–0945	105 white1	2359	Paz	attack Abu Ageila
0800–0945	105 white2	2326	Niv	ditto
0800–0945	105 white3	2335	Bodilewski	ditto
0800–0915	105 white4	2325	Ben-Nun	ditto

A second Squadron 105 formation was also tasked to attack the Abu Ageila sector and also experienced the absence of an FAC at Abu Ageila as well as difficulties in IFF. The formation therefore flew in the direction of El Arish and pinpointed a deployment of some 20

Squadron 113 pilot David Ivry at El Arish beside abandoned Sokol EGAF Number 311.

A destroyed Vampire dummy as photographed in a pen at El Arish after ILDF occupation.

tanks, about 10 tracked vehicles and approximately 10 other vehicles. Having already experienced IFF difficulties, the formation flew three passes for positive IFF and this may have enabled the enemy to better prepare for accurate aiming of AAA fire that hit three P-51s; white 2 was hit in the left fuel tanks and right wheel; white 3 was hit in the tail section and left fuel tanks; white 4 was hit in the oil system and Asaf Ben-Nun was forced to land in a field nearby NirIsaac. Damage to 2325 was classified as CAT4.

MOSQUITO WRITE-OFFS

0800–1005	110	2179	Orli/ Levy	attack El Arish
0800–1000	110	2181	Landau	ditto
0800–	110	2168	Gatmon	ditto
0800–	110	2177	Shemer	ditto
0800–1020	110	2171	Ash/Segal	ditto
0800–	110	Mosquito		ditto
0800–0955	110	2175	Levin/Hy	ditto
0800–	110	Mosquito	Eyal	ditto

Mosquitoes bombed El Arish camp and then strafed traffic along RADISH; Mosquito crews reported damage to El Arish camp and claimed the destruction of 13 vehicles. The EGDF returned fire and four Mosquitoes were hit. Among the damaged Mosquitoes were 2175 that RTBed safely, 2171 which got 15 hits – including one that pierced the undercarriage jack which resulted in a belly landing at Ramat David – and 2181 that was ground looped at Ramat David. Damage to both 2171 and 2181 was reported as CAT4.

TRAINERS' FIRST ATTACK

0800–	140	1169	Eshel	
		Yud176 attack Abu Ageila		
0800–	140	T-6	Peleg	ditto
0800–	140	T-6	Lapid	ditto
0800–	140	1165	Ophee	ditto

AIR3 issued MIOR176 at 0700. The MIOR stated that the ILDF was preparing to invade Abu Ageila and tasked Squadron 140 to attack enemy armor and fortifications in two waves, with TOT for the first wave at 0830 and for the second wave at 0845 but not later than 0900. Each wave was to include four T-6 trainers armed with 16 rockets per aircraft. The two formations were to fly from Teman Field to Abu Ageila – a distance of less than 100 kilometers – and back, at low altitude and to attack while in contact with FAC radio call sign FLY.

The T-6s apparently attempted to attack the Om Kattef fortifications. Tasking slow and vulnerable armed trainers to attack a well-defended and firmly-alerted fortification proved disastrous. All four T-6s were hit during the run-in to the target. Squadron 140 Commander Moshe Eshel was killed and the three remaining T-6s aborted the mission and RTBed. En route to Teman Field, Matanya Ophee was forced to belly land in a field nearby Zeelim, roughly halfway back from Abu Ageila to Teman Field.

PHOTOGRAPH JERUSALEM

0810–0910	101 green1	4545	Peled	patrol Sinai
0810–0910	101 green2	4552	Ronen	ditto
0810–0915	115	3517	Livneh/Dim	
		Yud159 photograph Jerusalem		
0820–0915	101red1	4543	Shapira	patrol Sinai
0820–0915	101red2	4563	Margalit	ditto

Squadron 101 green section did not encounter enemy aircraft so the pair attacked a train nearby El Arish. Squadron 101 red section did not encounter enemy aircraft either.

MIOR Yud159 tasked Squadron 115 to photograph the Jerusalem sector with a Squadron 117 Meteor equipped with a 24in camera; the mission produced 240 negatives and 720 prints that the Squadron 115 laboratory processed and printed from 0935, with distribution of data from 1330 and posting of prints from 1505. The total timeframe from ILAF/I requirement to the posting of prints was 12 hours and 25 minutes.

ROBUST OURAGANS

0820–	140	T-6	BarLev	
		Yud176 attack Abu Ageila		
0820–	140	T-6	Landesman	ditto
0820–	140	T-6	Safra	ditto
0820–	140	T-6	Yariv	ditto
0825–0920	115	Meteor		Yud156 photograph
0830–	113	Ouragan	Sharon	attack Abu Ageila
0830–	113	4042)	Rosen	ditto
0830–0910	113	4051	Sheffer	ditto
0830–	113	Ouragan	Erez	ditto

Brigade 7 – already at Abu Ageila, west of the Om Kattef fortifications – prepared for an advance in the direction of Jabel Libni in order to cut the road from Ismailia to Abu Ageila and complete the blockade of the Om Kattef fortifications. Meanwhile, Brigade 10 attacked Om Kattef from east to west. Tasking to attack Abu Ageila therefore referred to attacking the Om Kattef fortifications in support of Brigade 10.

Second Squadron's 140 formation tasked to fly MIOR Yud176 was retasked from attacking Om Kattef to interdiction west of Abu Ageila. Since Brigade 7 forces were already advancing from Abu Ageila, IFF was emphasized. The T-6 pilots pin-pointed a column of vehicles and flew an IFF pass but were unable to confirm identity of the column. In order to avoid a potential 'friendly fire' incident, the T-6 leader decided not to attack, flew to the Mediterranean Sea, jettisoned his rockets and returned to Teman Field.

The Ouragans were tasked to attack enemy forces along the road from Abu Ageila to El Arish. Ouragan pilots claimed the destruction of four armored vehicles but faced heavy return fire and the two Ouragans of the lead pair were damaged; one Ouragan was hit in a fuel tank and a flap; another was hit in the engine, the pilot seat and the belly of the aircraft. The Ouragan's reputation as an extremely robust aircraft capable of taking severe punishment in combat held up and all Ouragans RTBed safely.

STRAFE EGDF BRIGADE 1

0835–0930	101 pink1	Mystère	Morgan	patrol Sinai
0835–0930	101 pink2	4561	Golan	ditto
0835–	117	Meteor	Lavon	photograph EGDF Armor

Squadron 117 Meteor strafing an EGDF field kitchen in Sinai, reportedly taken by Mordehy Lavon on 31 October 1956. It is not known in which mission on that day this image was captured.

			Brigade 1 Jabel Libni/Bir Gafgafa	
0835–	117	3735	Zivoni	ditto
0840–	113		Ouragan Bareket	interdiction SPINACH
0840–	113		Ouragan Lidor	ditto

Meteors photographed the EGDF's Armor Brigade 1 which was advancing along the road from Bir Gafgafa to Jabel Libni and strafed it; AAA fire damaged one or two Meteors.

Ouragans also attacked the EGDF's Armor Brigade 1 between Bir Gafgafa and Jabel Libni and claimed the destruction of one Stalin tank, a hit on another tank and the destruction of several trucks. AAA fire damaged the two Ouragans; one was hit in the windshield, the other was holed by three rounds. On their way back to Hatzor, the Ouragan pilots spotted a train travelling from Gaza to Rafah but did not attack as they had run out of ammunition.

ENGAGEMENT OVER ABU AGEILA

0850–0955	101blue1	4580	Nevo	patrol Sinai
0850–0955	101blue2	4564	Zuk	ditto

Fighting focused on the Abu Ageila sector, where Brigade 7 was preparing to advance from Abu Ageila to Jabel Libni and Brigade 10 was attacking Om Kattef's fortifications; the Mitle sector – a sideshow right from the start with the sole objective to supply the Anglo-French coalition with a cause to act – calmed down as the EGDF failed in its Day 2 attack against Battalion 890, so EGDF troops deployed defensively in Mitle Pass and the ILDF ordered Brigade 202 – deployed east of Mitle Pass – not to attack the pass. Air activity focus also shifted from the Mitle sector to the Abu Ageila sector and it was over Abu Ageila that Squadron 101's blue section encountered MiGs.

Blue section patrolled over Abu Ageila at 30,000 feet when blue leader Jacob Nevo noted seven swept wing aircraft flying east at lower altitude. Swept wing aircraft could have been other ILAF Mysteres, EGAF MiGs or FRAF fighters; chances that these aircraft were Squadron 101 Mysteres were slim, because Squadron 101 Mysteres mostly operated in pairs, so it was more likely that these swept wing fighters were either EGAF MiGs or FRAF fighters, since by then FRAF squadrons in Israel, initially restricted to flying defensive patrols over Israel, had already initiated flying offensive operations over Sinai. Blue section descended to investigate and it was then that four of the swept wing fighters vanished from view, possibly flying into clouds. By then, the swept wing fighters were identified as EGAF MiGs and blue section attacked the three remaining MiGs, as Jacob Nevo reported:

> I glued to them and fired three short bursts but I did not hit. They spread into line astern. I followed the first [MiG] in a turn and the last among the three [MiGs] followed me; it closed to within firing range and opened fire so I left the first MiG and broke towards it... The MiG pilot got irritated and attempted nervous evasive action; he immediately turned hard right while diving and I followed him and opened fire. I did not hit. Throughout this combat only one of my guns fired. While shooting, I saw another MiG flying towards me on my right; he opened fire at 200 yards, broke at 50 yards and passed behind me. I broke this attack, reversed my aircraft and dived right behind him... I opened fire but I missed again... I decided to disengage.

A slightly different description of the same combat was presented in a post-war AIR4 analysis of EGAF operations during the Suez War:

> Mystère leader descended to low altitude in order to accomplish IFF and identified them as MiGs. While in pursuit after seven aircraft, four [MiGs] were 'lost' and three [MiGs] remained. The Mystère caught up with them. The MiGs turned left in slight climb as they probably noticed our aircraft. As the Mystère got closer, the MiGs spread into line astern with MiG Number 1 trying to follow the Mystère that attacked the third MiG. The MiG fired without deflection and the Mystère pilot said that he was able to notice it during combat.

ROCKETS VERSUS COMMUNICATION LINE

0850–	113		Ouragan Zahavi	attack Abu Ageila sector
0850–	113		Ouragan Furman	ditto
0900–	113	4073	Kishon	attack Abu Ageila sector
0900–	113		Ouragan Yariv	ditto

Squadron 113 pilots Menahem Zahavi and Giora Furman were tasked to cut an underground communication line with rockets, a bizarre tasking that failed as the communication line was not cut.

DITCHING AT BARDAVIL

0910–1000	101 khaki1	4546	Lev	patrol Sinai
0910–1000	101 khaki2	4592	Lapidot	ditto

A short while after Squadron 101's blue section disengaged from its inconclusive combat over Abu Ageila, the two Mysteres linked-up with khaki section. It was then that Mystère pilots encountered two MiG-15s, as Jacob Nevo reported:

> Within a short while I had the upper hand over one of them; a brief burst from 600 yards; a miss. Second burst from 400 [yards]; a miss. For the third burst I waited until I closed to 200 yards and then I opened fire.
> The MiG was hit, one of the wings exploded and a large piece of structure disintegrated. Black smoke poured out of it but the Egyptian pilot did not lose control of the MiG. It looked like he was planning an emergency landing at ElArish... I closed [range] to within 100 yards... squeezed trigger but nothing happened. I called Number 2... but he was also out of ammunition... The MiG flew along coastline in direction of Port Said.

Out of ammunition and short on fuel, the Mysteres disengaged and RTBed. The fate of the damaged MiG-15 was unknown, yet at 1000, the ILDF reported to AIR3, presumably a report based on ILDF/I information, that the EGDF's Armor Brigade 1 was 75 kilometers east of Bir Gafgafa and that one EGDF MiG had been shot down. AIR4 Intelligence Report Number 8, issued at 1130, stated:

> MiG-15 aircraft was destroyed during emergency landing at El Arish.

Post-war, the ILDF salvaged a MiG-15 that ditched at Bardavil, along the Sinai coastline between El Arish and Port Said. The ditched MiG-15 was fairly intact apart from a seriously damaged right wing. The location of the MiG-15 and the damage it sustained – Mystère 80 fired with only one gun – supported the combat report of Jacob Nevo and the ILAF credited him with a kill. AMV1 identified the EGAF pilot flying the MiG-15 that was damaged in combat and then ditched at Bardavil as Abed el Rahman Muharram.

Squadron 101 blue and khaki pilots - left to right: Amos Lapidot, Zorik Lev, Jacob Nevo and Josef Zuk - after air combat on 31 October 1956.

Post-war, ILAF recovered this MiG-15 from Bardavil; the MiG-15 was initially delivered to Tel Nof for inspection and survey of damage in order to evaluate the option to fly the MiG-15. Damage was too extensive and eventually the MiG-15 was transferred to Hatzor for display; it is still on display at Hatzor beside a Mystère painted as 4580, the Mystère that Jacob Nevo flew on 31 October 1956 when he most likely engaged the MiG-15 that was forced to land at Bardavil.

MITLE

0910 –	113		Ouragan	Halivni	attack Mitle sector
0910 –1020	113	4029		Ivry	ditto
0920 –	113	4070		Agassi	attack Mitle sector
0920 –	113		Ouragan	Ayalon	ditto

The ILDF focus shifted from Brigade 202 and the Mitle sector to Division 38 and the Abu Ageila sector, but the ILAF also continued to attack the EGDF west of Brigade 202.

ILAF credited Jacob Nevo with one MiG-15 kill over El Arish, in Mystère 80, on 31 October 1956.

Squadron 105 pilot Akiva Pressman flew P-51 54 as blue 3 on 31 October 1956 morning. The weary-looking P-51 was photographed with ILAF Suez War IFF stripes version 1.

SPINACH

0920–	117	Meteor	Yoeli	interdiction SPINACH
0920–	117	Meteor	Sapir	ditto
0920–	117	Meteor	Altman	ditto
0920–	117	Meteor	Gat	ditto

Squadron 117 Meteor pilots strafed targets along SPINACH, where the EGDF's Armor Brigade 1 advanced for an expected clash with Brigade 7, which did not yet depart Abu Ageila in the direction of Jabel Libni. Meteor pilots claimed the destruction of up to ten vehicles, while Egyptian return fire lightly damaged three Meteors.

FROM FOUR TO TWO

0925–1140	105blue1 2333	Hagani	interdiction Sinai
0925–0940	105blue2 2328	Shaked	ditto
0940–1020	105blue3 2354	Pressman	ditto
0925–1140	105blue4 2336	Helman	ditto

Squadron 105 blue was planned to interdict as a four-ship formation but actually accomplished the mission as a pair; blue 3 took off late, probably due to some kind of malfunction, and was then forced to

RTB, while blue 2 was forced to abort the mission, en route from Ramat David to Sinai, diverted to Hatzor and landed there.

The blue pair attacked armor along the road from Bir Gafgafa to Abu Ageila with napalm and strafing, the P-51 pilots claiming the destruction of three tanks and one truck; return fire damaged 2333 in the tail section. On their way back, they sighted tanks advancing from El Arish to Abu Ageila but could not attack as they had already ran out of ammunition.

BLACK VERSUS MIGS OVER BIR HAMA

0940–1025	101gold1	4530	Gonen	patrol Sinai
0940–1025	101gold2	4533	Dekel	ditto
0940–	113	Ouragan	Harlev	interdiction Sinai
0940–	113	Ouragan	Dan	ditto
0945–1045	101 black1	4590	Gilboa	patrol Sinai
0945–1045	101 black2	4585	Shadmi	ditto

Squadron 101's black section reportedly encountered seven MiGs near Bir Hama and during the subsequent combat a Mystère pilot claimed a hit, but the engagement was inconclusive. This report may be in error – possibly related to the wrong pair; it probably related to Squadron 101's black section that departed Hatzor at 1100 – since both Shabtai Gilboa and Ohad Shadmi did not mention an engagement with enemy aircraft and both reported a patrol over Mitle and strafing enemy vehicles, while Shadmi reported:

> Hit a telephone line nearby Mitle, downed a pole and RTB with five wires on wing.

SQUADRON 116 FIRST STRIKE

0950–1145	116	2303	Yavneh	interdiction SPINACH
0950–	116	P-51	Burstein	ditto
0950–1240	116	2330	Etkes	ditto
0950–	116	2320	Rafaeli	ditto
0950–	116	2352	Barak	ditto
0950–	116	P-51	Bloch	ditto

Tasked to attack the EGDF's Armor Brigade 1 along SPINACH, the six P-51s flew at low altitude and passed near an Egyptian fortification that opened fire at the P-51s and hit the second pair. Both Jonathan Etkes – whose aircraft was hit in the right wing, a hit that dropped the three rockets attached to that wing – and Jacob Rafaeli pressed ahead but, four minutes later, the engine of 2320 succumbed to damage and Rafaeli was forced to land somewhere near Jabel Libni, an area still in Egyptian hands. Rafaeli jettisoned the two napalm canisters prior to landing but landed on the six rockets. Etkes aborted the mission and, regardless of damage to his own aircraft, orbited overhead until 1225 while trying to contact ILDF units in order to arrange a rescue. Jonathan Etkes reported:

> On our way to target, Jabel Libni, over Abu Ageila fortifications, my wingman Jacob Rafaeli was hit and landed at map reference... as a result of a round in radiator. I watched over him for as long as I could and later that day an ILDF command car picked him up.

Squadron 116 servicemen prepare a P-51 for mission, with two bombs and six rockets, during the Suez War. This photo was taken after 0600 on 2 November 1956 as the P-51 is marked with ILAF Suez War IFF stripes version 2.

Squadron 116 P-51s in flight. This photo was taken after 0600 on 2 November 1956 as P-51 is marked with ILAF Suez War IFF stripes version 2.

Luckily for Rafaeli, Brigade 7's Battalion 52 started to advance from Abu Ageila to Jabel Libni at 1000 and occupied Jabel Libni junction circa 1400. The rescue of Rafaeli was accomplished circa 1630; the pilot was transported to Quseima and Beer Sheba, from where he was flown back to Tel Nof.

The other four P-51s pressed ahead and claimed the destruction of one tank and two Jeeps.

EL ARISH RADAR STATION

1010–	117	Meteor	Ben Aaron	attack RADAR station El Arish
1010–1050	117	3606	Sarig	ditto
1010–1055	117	3603)	Kaspit	ditto
1010–1040	117	3602	Yahalom	ditto

EGAF activity prompted the ILAF to task Squadron 117 to attack a radar station near El Arish in order to degrade the efficiency of EGAF operations over north Sinai. The Meteors strafed the target but it turned out that the target was a dummy station; the real radar station would fall into ILDF hands practically intact.

SECOND SEXTET

1020–	116	P-51	Zeelon	interdiction SPINACH
1020–1250	116	2312	Fredilis	ditto
1020–	116	P-51	Geva	ditto
1020–	116	P-51	Kohorn	ditto
1020–	116	P-51	Sharon	ditto
1020–	116	P-51	Hativa	ditto

Uniquely, Squadron 116 launched six-ship formations to interdict the EGDF's Armor Brigade 1 in order to weaken the Egyptian unit prior to its expected clash with Brigade 7. Squadron 116's second sextet, tasked to interdict Armor Brigade 1, experienced an eventful mission. First they encountered the P-51 of Jonathan Etkes, orbiting over the landing site of Jacob Rafaeli near Jabel Libni. They then wandered somewhat south, to Bir Hasana, along CARROT. While Brigade 7's Battalion 52 advanced from Abu Ageila to Jabel Libni along SPINACH, Brigade 7's Battalion 9 advanced from Abu Ageila to Bir Hasana along CARROT. At the time, Battalion 9 had already

arrived at Bir Hasana and it was there that the P-51 pilots observed three Mosquitoes supposedly attacking Battalion 9. The P-51 leader radioed to the Mosquito leader to ceasefire and the two formations flew apart, with the P-51s returning north to SPINACH.

Along SPINACH, between Bir Hama and Bir Gafgafa, the P-51s pinpointed an element of the EGDF's Armor Brigade 1 and attacked with napalm, rockets and guns. The six P-51s reportedly exhausted all ammunition, except for seven rockets that failed to launch, in several passes but the combined claim was destruction of two tanks and two vehicles; a later Squadron 116 source reported claims of the destruction of five vehicles and no tanks at all. Egyptian return fire hit one P-51 that suffered very light damage – a small caliber hole – and RTBed.

SOMEONE SHOUTED

1035–	110	Mosquito	Bavli	interdiction SPINACH
1035–	110	Mosquito	Amiran	ditto
1035–	110	Mosquito	Fuchs	ditto

The Mosquitoes reportedly attacked in the Bir Hama sector and claimed the destruction of one tank, one tracked vehicle and six other vehicles. However, the Mosquitoes abruptly aborted the attack, as one of the pilots reported:

> We flew rocketry passes and strafed vehicles until someone shouted to us that we were attacking our forces; we stopped the attack and RTBed.

The someone who shouted was a Squadron 116 P-51 pilot, presumably the leader of the second sextet. The P-51 pilots reported that they encountered the Mosquitoes over Bir Hasana. Brigade 7's Battalion 9 Deputy Commander reported that at about 1030, when Battalion 9 prepared to attack Bir Hasana, four 'friendly' Ouragans attacked Battalion 9 – which had no attached FAC – and injured two troops, but the same source did not mention a Mosquito attack and there should have been a distinct difference between four Ouragans and three Mosquitoes, even from the perspective of ILDF troops. It is also true that Battalion 9 reported the 'friendly fire' incident as occurring at 1030 while reported take-off time for the

Squadron 110 servicemen maintain a Mosquito at Ramat David during the Suez War. The Mosquito's common configuration during the Suez War was bombs and rockets.

Command South Chief of Staff Rehavam Zeevi (left) and Brigade 202 Commander Ariel Sharon (right) in front of Squadron 100 Piper 38 during discussion at JAMAICA on 31 October 1956.

three Mosquitoes was 1035, but such a discrepancy should be given less weight due to the many timing errors in ILDF reports during wartime. In any case, there were no ILDF troops at Bir Hama at that time; Brigade 7's Battalion 52 departed Jabel Libni for Bir Hama at 1600 and arrived at Bir Hama at 2000; and Brigade 7's Battalion 9 advanced from Bir Hasana to Bir Hama during the afternoon and evening hours, linked up with Battalion 52 and the two battalions parked overnight at Bir Hama.

Available information, at this point, cannot lift the fog of war that covers timing, place and IFF. When was Battalion 9 attacked by 'friendly' aircraft? Where did the Mosquitoes attack? Whom did the Mosquitoes attack, Egyptians or Israelis? In any case, the Mosquitoes' claims do not fit with reported damage to Battalion 9.

EIGHT MIGS OVER SINAI

1050–1140	101 white1	4547	Bar	patrol Sinai
1050–1140	101 white2	4535	BetOn	ditto

Squadron 101's white section reportedly encountered eight MiGs but managed to disengage, a phrasing that may suggest that no actual air combat took place. The ILDF noted, at 1100, that enemy aircraft attacked Brigade 202, so the sighted MiGs may have been involved in EGAF action against Brigade 202, either actually attacking or acting as cover to attack aircraft.

PATROL MITLE

	100	0438		Beer Sheba–Mitle

The ILDF focus shifted from Brigade 202 operations along PEPPER to Division 38's offensive at SPINACH sector. The drop of Battalion 890 at JAMAICA, advance of Brigade 202 along PEPPER and eventual link-up at JAMAICA did not involve heavy fighting and did not have a profound impact upon the ILDF campaign, but was of utmost political importance as it gave Anglo-French forces a cause for intervention in order to secure safety of shipping in the Suez Canal. Though the Anglo-French offensive was not launched yet – because it was delayed for 24 hours from the evening of 30 October to the evening of 31 October – the Brigade 202 mission to create a cause had been accomplished.

After Battalion 890 – and/or ILAF support – repelled the EGDF attack from Mitle Pass to JAMAICA, from west to east, on 30 October, and after Brigade 202 linked up with Battalion 890, the situation seemed static, with Brigade 202 at JAMAICA and the opposing Egyptian forces at Mitle Pass, west of JAMAICA. The only actions were occasional EGAF strikes and the ILDF had already ordered Brigade 202 not to attack the EGDF deployment in the Mitle Pass.

Circa 1100, Command South Chief of Staff Rehavam Zeevi flew from Command South HQ at Beer Sheba, in a Squadron 100 Piper, to visit Brigade 202 at JAMAICA and to emphasize the ILDF order not to advance west. Zeevi reportedly repeated and stressed the ILDF order so Brigade 202 Commander Ariel Sharon asked permission to patrol Mitle; Zeevi authorized this. However, when Zeevi departed JAMAICA, in the Piper, he noticed that the force getting organized to patrol Mitle was large; in fact, the patrol force was a column that composed a Battalion 88 company, AMX-13 tanks company, second Battalion 88 company, mortars battery, the Brigade 202 scout unit and a medical unit; the ILAF post-war report indicated that Brigade 202 ALO Israel Lahav and FAC Dov Matos were also among the patrol forces in FAC Mobile Number 24.

Was it a force preparing to patrol Mitle for evaluation or was it a force preparing to attack Mitle for occupation? Either way, the Brigade 202 patrol/attack force departed JAMAICA at 1230 and headed west to the Mitle Pass.

SEVEN MIGS OVER BIR HAMA

1100–1140	113	4050	Sheffer	interdiction SPINACH
1100–	113	Ouragan	Erez	ditto
1100–	117	3735	Zivoni	interdiction El Arish
1100–	117	Meteor	Lavon	ditto
1110–1235	101 black1	4594	Alon	patrol Sinai
1110–1235	101 black2	4530	Avneri	ditto

Ouragan pilots attacked in the Bir Hama sector. Meteor pilots spotted a static train near Rafah and strafed it, with no apparent results.

Squadron 101 pilot Dror Avneri engaged MiGs in Mystère 30 on 31 October 1956. This photo was taken after the introduction of ILAF Suez War IFF stripes version 2 from 0600 on 2 November 1956.

The second strike thus far unearthed against Vampire dummies at El Arish was some time after 1130 on 31 October 1956, when two Meteors strafed the realistic dummies.

IOKR stated that Squadron 101's black section – Joe Alon and Dror Avneri – encountered four MiGs over Bir Hama and during the subsequent engagement the Mysteres did not hit and were not hit. Alon reported:

Air combat versus seven MiGs with Avneri.

Avneri added:

At the end of our patrol over Sinai we encountered MiGs that attacked two Ouragans; we entered combat and were forced to disengage due to low fuel state. My engine flamed out at 5,000 feet [altitude] over somewhere in between Rafah and Gaza; I performed successful emergency landing at base.

IOKR may have been in error, possibly a mix-up with the report that Squadron 101 black that departed Hatzor at 0945 – Shabtai Gilboa and Ohad Shadmi – engaged seven MiGs over Bir Hama and that one of the black pilots hit a MiG. Neither Alon nor Avneri mentioned a hit on an enemy aircraft.

EGDF ARMOR BRIGADE 1 LOSS

1120–	113	Ouragan	Hod	interdiction/support SPINACH
1120–	113	Ouragan	Lidor	ditto
1120–	117	3733	Yoeli	interdiction El Arish
1120–	117	Meteor	Gat	ditto
1120–	117	Meteor	Altman	attack El Arish airfield
1120–	117	Meteor	Sapir	ditto

In line with the shift of emphasis from PEPPER to SPINACH, the ILDF ordered AIR3, at 1115, to transfer emphasis of support from Brigade 202 – operating along PEPPER – to Brigade 7 – advancing along SPINACH – as well as to emphasize interdiction against the EGDF's Armor Brigade 1 that was advancing from west to east along SPINACH, on a collision course with Brigade 7.

The Squadron 113 Ouragan pair claimed to have destroyed one Stalin tank along SPINACH, near Bir Hama.

Squadron 117 Meteor pilots Aaron Yoeli and Uri Gat strafed vehicles near El Arish. Egyptian fire hit the lead Meteor and injured Yoeli in his hand, but Yoeli RTBed. Meanwhile, the other Meteor pair strafed Vampires – the dummy Vampires – at El Arish, where Egyptian fire hit the Meteor of Shlomo Sapir, who was forced to perform SEL at Hatzor.

The ILAF impact upon the EGDF's Armor Brigade 1 – the main Egyptian armor fist in Sinai – was certainly significant even though the ILAF did not secure air superiority over Sinai and the EGAF operated in large numbers over Sinai. ILDF/I reported, at 1125, that Armor Brigade 1 had lost 91 vehicles of all types until then. Five minutes later, at 1130, the ILDF noted an ILDF/I listening report that Armor Brigade 1 reported the loss of 81 vehicles until then. Regardless of what was obviously some kind of typo, the EGDF's Armor Brigade 1 loss of 80 or 90 vehicles had been a significant blow to the strongest EGDF unit in Sinai and a major accomplishment for the ILDF that can be attributed in entirety to the ILAF, since Armor Brigade 1 did not yet engage the ILDF's Brigade 7 or any other ILDF unit.

ILDF accomplishments – Brigade 202's advance along PEPPER and link-up with Battalion 890 at JAMAICA, and the Brigade 7 offensive along SPINACH and CARROT – outweighed its failures – notably Brigade 10's failed attack against the Om Kattef fortifications – and more accomplishments could have been expected. Thus Runway Branch Unit 731 was activated at Tel Nof in line with the AIR1 organization order issued at 1130. Ten minutes later, at 1140, Tel Nof reported that Runway Unit 721 was preparing for its mission. Runway Branch Unit 731 was activated with tasking for assignment to Brigade 202, that had already been attached with Runway Unit 625 but by then was planned to operate two emergency airfields, one at Nekhel and one at JAMAICA. Runway Unit 721 was tasked to operate from Bir Hama airfield, which at the time had not been occupied, but by then it was clear that the next objective for Brigade 7 was the advance of Battalion 52 from Jabel Libni to Bir Hama and advance of Battalion 9 from Bir Hasana to Bir Hama.

MIGS OVER JABEL LIBNI

| 1140–1250 | 101 silver1 | 4584 | Egozi | patrol Sinai |
| 1140–1250 | 101 silver2 | 4550 | Shavit | ditto |

IOKR indicated that Squadron 101's silver section – Shy Egozi and Aaron Shavit – engaged several MiGs, inconclusively, over Jabel Libni but, thus far, no original documents have been unearthed to support IOKR.

THREE P-51S OVER SPINACH

1140–1340	105red1	2339	Kopel	interdiction SPINACH
1140–1345	105red2	2310	Maor	ditto
1140–1335	105red3	2331	Pressman	ditto
	105red4		Melamed	abort before take off

Tasked to attack the EGDF's Armor Brigade 1 along SPINACH as a four-ship formation, Squadron 105's red section departed Ramat David as a three-ship formation and attacked Armor Brigade 1 along the sector from Bir Hama to Bir Gafgafa. The three P-51 pilots claimed the destruction of four tanks, six tracked vehicles and one large communication vehicle.

FIVE P-51S OVER SPINACH

1140–1300	116	P-51	Yoffe	interdiction SPINACH
1140–1300	116	P-51	Hasson	ditto
1140–1300	116	P-51	Naveh	ditto
1140–	116	2306	Schlesinger	ditto
1140–	116	2304	Cohen	ditto

AIR3 Chief Abraham Yoffe arrived at Tel Nof from ILAF HQ at Ramla to lead a Squadron 116 five-ship formation tasked to attack Armor Brigade 1 along SPINACH, between Bir Hama and Bir Gafgafa. Each P-51 was armed with two napalm canisters and six rockets. The debrief form summed up the mission:

> We passed over Halutza Sands, crossed CHAIR and arrived at STOOL. We saw a convoy along road roughly halfway between HOLLAND and FRANCE; convoy included trucks and troops with helmets. When we arrived, trucks stopped and troops fled. We did not observe IFF marks; they headed south-east, at least 30 vehicles. We arrived north of AUSTRIA... and from there flew straight south to SPINACH. Along SPINACH we observed a long convoy. We flew over convoy and noted tanks, half-tracks, trucks and Jeeps; the convoy stretched from AUSTRIA up to a point some ten kilometers east of Bir Gafgafa. We did not see IFF marks. The tanks were very big with large guns, long barrels and the turrets of the tanks were positioned forward rather than in the middle [of the hull, therefore hinting at T-34 and/or Stalin tanks]. We flew to Point 14 [Jabal Yalak] where we got organized in combat formation, turned north and attacked tanks and one half-track with napalm. We hit two tanks and one half-track. We turned [overhead] to assess [damage]... they were burning. We then flew to SPINACH 7 [Bir Rod Salam] where there was a large deployment of concentrated tanks, about 15, with some 25 to 30 vehicles and trucked vehicles around them. We attacked with rockets and hit two tanks, two vehicles and one half-track. The troops dispersed and took cover in the fields, away from the convoy... We then strafed and hit... AAA gun... seven

trucks and two Jeeps. We exhausted ammunition and RTBed along SPINACH, flying south of the road. Three [AAA] guns were noted at the north-west corner between TABLE and SPINACH, on the hills... [these AAA guns opened fire and] a shell exploded nearby Yoffe... On our way back, while flying over Rehovot in the Negev, Number 4 reported engine vibrations and that he was performing an emergency landing. Yoffe ordered Number 5 to escort Number 4 and the rest RTBed.

IOKR stated that the five P-51 pilots claimed the destruction of four tanks, three tracked vehicles, nine trucks, three vehicles and one AAA gun, while a Squadron 116 source indicated that the five P-51 pilots claimed to have destroyed two tanks, one AAA gun and 11 vehicles. During the attack, Egyptian fire holed a fuel tank in the P-51 that Cheetah Cohen flew, but the pilot switched tanks and pressed ahead.

Uri Schlesinger attempted an emergency landing but 2306 crashed and Schlesinger was killed. Cheetah Cohen escorted Schlesinger and then landed at Teman Field, where he reported to ILAF Commander Dan Tolkowsky, who was visiting Squadron 140 in the wake of the loss of Squadron 140 Commander Moshe Eshel earlier that morning; the ILAF Commander handed over command of Squadron 140 to Ovadia Nachman, who took over as Squadron 140 Commander (Acting).

TWO OURAGANS VERSUS EIGHT MIGS

| 1150– | 113 | 4061 | Sharon | interdiction SPINACH |
| 1150– | 113 | | Ouragan Rosen | ditto |

MiGs intercepted the two Ouragans, as Ran Sharon reported:

> Suddenly I heard my wingman shouting 'Number 1, break, MiGs are right behind you'. I broke. Then I saw that three MiGs were behind my wingman so I yelled to him 'break, they are right behind you'. He broke. Two MiGs followed me. Meanwhile, Rosen turned with his MiGs and after half a full turn positioned himself behind a MiG, but two other MiGs followed him. I entered scissors with a MiG, and while at it got as close as ten meters and even less... I accomplished an edge over that MiG but another MiG was right behind me. No

Squadron 113 pilot Ran Sharon in front of Ouragan 44.

Squadron 103 C-47 at JAMAICA. C-47s landed at JAMAICA from the night of 31 October to 1 November 1956, while daylight flights of Squadron 103 airlifters started on 2 November 1956, by which time ILAF aircraft were marked with Suez War IFF stripes version 2, as illustrated.

A Squadron 100 Piper flying over ILDF vehicles, reportedly in Sinai during the Suez War, in which case it is believed that poles along the road are communication lines of the same type that ILAF P-51s were tasked to cut during Day 1 and 2.

wonder, there were eight MiGs and only two of us. I performed a barrel roll and a split S in the hope that he would follow me and fly into the ground, but he did not follow me. By then I was at low altitude and running out of fuel because the wingtip tanks did not transfer fuel [due to a malfunction] so I started to disengage. I realized that I would not make it back to base. I located a convenient place for an emergency landing and landed.

Ouragan 61 was classed as CAT3 and was duly repaired. Meanwhile, a MiG hit the other Ouragan but Avinoam Rosen RTBed.

JAMAICA AIRLIFT READINESS

| 1200– | 117 | Meteor | Alroy | photograph Abu Ageila (???) |

IOKR mentioned a Squadron 117 reconnaissance mission that departed Tel Nof at 1200 but failed to yield photographic products due to a malfunctioning camera. A post-war list of reconnaissance missions included four missions flown on 31 October, but none of these took-off at 1200, none of these photographed Abu Ageila and all four of these listed reconnaissance missions produced negatives and prints, so either this mission was not included in the post-war list because it failed or there is an error in IOKR.

Also at 1200, the ILDF noted that a Brigade 11 battalion was ready to move from Lod to Tel Nof for onwards airlift to Nekhel in order to replace Brigade 202's Battalion 88; at exactly the same time, Battalion 88 was preparing to patrol Mitle. Ten minutes later, at 1210, Tel Nof Operations ordered Squadron 103 to place on readiness two C-47s – 1412 and 1414 – and two crews – with Michael Ben-Josef in command of the lead crew – for airlift mission to JAMAICA.

RED VERSUS MIGS

1220–	113		Ouragan	Zahavi	interdiction SPINACH
1220–	113		Ouragan	Furman	ditto
1230–1345	101 green1	4561		Peled	patrol Sinai
1230–1345	101 green2	4562		Ronen	ditto

Squadron 113 pilot David Ivry flew Ouragan 42 to interdict RADISH on 31 October 1956; 4042 was photographed after 0600 on 2 November 1956, as it is marked with ILAF Suez War IFF stripes version 2.

| 1230–1350 | 101red1 | 4549 | Shapira | patrol Sinai |
| 1230–1350 | 101red2 | 4563 | Margalit | ditto |

Squadron 101's red section encountered four MiGs over Jabel Libni and an inconclusive combat followed.

ENEMY FIRE HITS PIPER

| 1230–1515 | 100 | 0434 | Sirotkin/ Nitzana–Nitzana scout |

Squadron 100 Flight, supporting Division 77, operated from Nitzana and was tasked by Command South, so there was no AIR3 MIOR issued prior to this mission; the tasking was reconnaissance of the Abu Ageila sector, communication with ILDF units in the Abu Ageila sector and observation of the road between Abu Ageila and Bir Hasana. Paltiel Sirotkin reported in debrief:

As I arrived over [ILDF] attacking force; enemy forces opened fire from machine guns. I heard that the aircraft was hit so I immediately turned and landed. Afterwards I pressed ahead because I decided that the hits would not prevent me from pressing ahead and the mission was important.

Post-flight inspection revealed that three rounds hit the Piper.

OURAGANS OVER SPINACH AND RADISH

Time	Sqn	No.	Pilot	Mission
1240–	113		Ouragan Halivni	interdiction Abu Ageila/El Arish
1240–1320	113	4042	Ivry	ditto
1240–	113	4071	Kishon	interdiction Bir Hama/Bir Gafgafa
1240–	113		Ouragan Yariv	ditto

Ouragan pilots reported some 50 tanks along SPINACH between Bir Hama and Bir Gafgafa and no traffic along RADISH between El Arish and Qantara. Also noted were MiGs in patrol over the sector from Bir Hama to Bir Gafgafa.

METEORS OVER STOOL

Time	Sqn	No.	Pilot	Mission
1250–	117	3735	Zivoni	interdiction Abu Ageila/El Arish
1250–1330	117	3606	Sarig	ditto
1250–	117	Meteor	Lavon	ditto
1250–1330	117	3605	Yahalom	ditto

The Squadron 117 pilots were tasked to attack, along STOOL between Abu Ageila and Bir Lahfan and along TABLE between Bir Lahfan and El Arish, enemy forces that were in contact with Brigade 7's Battalion 82. The Meteor pilots strafed and claimed to have destroyed seven tanks, seven half-tracks and three vehicles. ILAF post-war BDA research concluded that strafing probably never destroyed a tank during the Suez War, though in some cases it managed to disable tanks. Return fire damaged 3605 with a single 0.303in round that holed a fuel tank.

ARMED TRAINERS OVER STOOL AND TABLE

Time	Sqn	No.	Pilot	Mission
1250–	140	1144	Gideoni	interdiction Abu Ageila/El Arish
1250–	140	T-6	Peled	ditto
1250–	140	T-6	Bar Lev	ditto
1250–	140	T-6	Yarom	ditto
1250–	140	T-6	Ben Zvi	interdiction Abu Ageila/El Arish
1250–	140	T-6	Marcus	ditto
1250–	140	T-6	Vronski	ditto
1250–	140	T-6	Elisha	ditto

Also attacking along STOOL – between Abu Ageila and Bir Lahfan – and TABLE – between Bir Lahfan and El Arish – were two Squadron 140 four-ship formations. The eight T-6 pilots attacked with rockets and claimed the destruction of one armored vehicle, one tracked vehicle and five other vehicles.

A WALK IN THE DESERT

Time	Sqn	No.	Pilot	Mission
1300–1410	105 white1	2319	Paz	interdiction Jabel Libni/Bir Gafgafa
1300–1520	105 white2	2359	Dagan	ditto
	105 white3	2336	Bodilewski	ditto
1300–1520	105 white4	2333	Melamed	ditto

Squadron 105's white section departed Ramat David as three-

Reportedly the landing site of P-51 19 somewhere west of Bir Hasana.

ILDF troops inspect Squadron 116 P-51 19 that Eldad Paz landed in Sinai on 31 October 1956; 2319 is painted with ILAF Suez War IFF stripes version 1.

P-51 19 belly landed with rockets - a detached rocket points at the aircraft. At the time of the Suez War, ILAF combat aircraft could RTB with rockets but bombs and napalm canisters had to be jettisoned if the mission had to be aborted; rockets were not jettisoned with bombs but had to be launched separately.

ship because white 3 had to abort the mission prior to take-off. The three P-51 pilots attacked the EGDF's Armor Brigade 1 along SPINACH between Bir Hama and Bir Gafgafa, where some 40 tanks and additional vehicles were spotted. IOKR indicated that white claimed to have destroyed three tanks, one tanker and two trucks, but Egyptian fire hit white 1, as Eldad Paz reported:

> We passed over Jabel Libni and Bir Hama before we saw Egyptian vehicles along the road and descended to attack. I placed a napalm on top of an Egyptian tank... It was a good hit, I saw it engulfed in flames. Not far behind this tank was an AAA gun on a trailer. I dropped on it my second napalm but the moment I released [the] napalm, I saw that the gun was firing right at me even though I flew very low. I sensed

that the aircraft was rocking and the cockpit was immediately filled with white warm smoke. I pulled up and turned. I asked my wingman what he saw. He answered that smoke was pouring out of my engine. I noted that oil pressure dropped and I realized that I was hit in the radiator... I managed to climb to 1,300 feet before I switched off the engine... I ejected canopy... looked down and saw a field more or less suitable for landing... I belly landed... There were quite rough bumps; the aircraft rolled and bumped along 150 meters or so. After it stopped I released harness and jumped outside... Before our departure, we were told not to attack Bir Hasana area because there was a possibility that our forces were already there, so I decided to walk to there [Bir Hasana] at night. I had another reason for this. There is a well there [at Bir Hasana] and I knew that I would not be able to survive without water.

Eldad Paz waited for nightfall and then walked from the landing site – south-west to Bir Hama and on south side of SPINACH – to Bir Hasana. Paz arrived at Bir Hasana on the morning of 1 November, but by then Battalion 9 had already advanced to Bir Hama so there were no ILDF troops at Bir Hasana and Paz continued his desert march north to Jabel Libni, where he finally linked-up with ILDF troops more than 30 hours after landing in the desert.

OURAGAN VERSUS MIG

1310–1410	101pink1	4545	Morgan	patrol Sinai
1310–1410	101pink2	4552	Golan	ditto
1310–1410	113	4043	Sheffer	interdiction SPINACH
1310–	113		Ouragan Erez	ditto
1310–1350	113	4028	Agassi	interdiction SPINACH
1310–1350	113		Ouragan Ayalon	ditto

The Mystère pair that was tasked to patrol Sinai and look for enemy aircraft did not encounter any. The Squadron 113 pair with Samuel Sheffer as leader operated over the Bir Gafgafa sector and also did not encounter enemy aircraft. The Squadron 113 pair with Jacob Agassi as leader operated over the Abu Ageila sector and encountered enemy aircraft. Jacob Agassi reported:

The MiGs attacked me and my wingman. We turned with them and requested help from Mysteres but they were probably busy with other MiGs. The MiG-17 was much faster [but] its radius of turn was larger so it was unable to shoot at us. I ordered my wingman to reverse his turn and then I [opened fire and] hit the MiG for the first time. I ordered my wingman to disengage, chased the MiG and from a range of 200 meters I [opened fire and] hit him in the engine and the left wing. Since I knew that there were no more MiGs around, I decided to dive to deck with maximum throttle [in order to disengage]. When I left the MiG-17 it was smoking heavily.

PXNE and AMV1 presented recollections of MiG-15 pilot Farouk el Gazawi that may match the engagement with Agassi and Ayalon. Gazawi's claim that he remained alone fits in with Agassi reporting fighting a single MiG; perhaps all MiGs attacked in a first pass and only Gazawi remained for a dogfight. Gazawi thought that

Ouragan 28 had been painted with a kill marking in the wake of the 31 October 1956 air combat - the other kill marking dated back to April 1956 - but the ILAF did not credit a kill to Jacob Agassi.

he attacked the Ouragan leader and was attacked by the Ouragan wingman, but he probably attacked the Ouragan wingman and was attacked by the leader. Gazawi reported being hit twice and Agassi reported hitting the MiG twice; in between the hits, Gazawi reported that the Ouragan he was following reversed, while Agassi reported that between the hits he ordered his wingman to disengage. Gazawi described a hole in the wing and damage to the fuselage; Agassi reported hitting the engine and left wing.

Gazawi landed in his damaged MiG but claimed that the Ouragan he attacked crash-landed, a claim that is most likely a post-war mix-up as both Agassi and Ayalon returned to Hatzor while the only Ouragan to perform an emergency landing in a field – not a crash landing – was Ouragan 61, which Ran Sharon landed a short while earlier.

ALL THE WAY BACK TO RAMAT DAVID

1310–1500	110	2126)	Orli/Hy	interdiction RADISH
1310–	110		Mosquito Landau	ditto
1310–1505	110	2168	Gatmon/Alber	ditto
1310–	110	2184	Shemer	ditto

The four Mosquitoes bombed El Arish and hit hangars at El Arish airfield. IOKR indicated that the Mosquitoes then – or also – attacked a static train near El Arish, while formation leader Dave Orli reported that they then interdicted traffic along the road from El Arish to

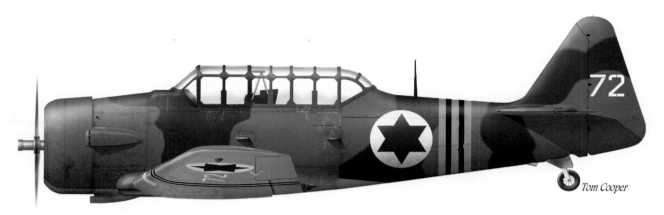

Prior to the Sinai Campaign of 1956, the Flying School of the IDF/AF formed the 'Golden Eagle' Squadron, equipped with AT-6 Harvards converted for ground-attack missions and flown by instructors. All the aircraft were painted in standardised colours including brown (close to RAL 8000) and blue (close to RAL 5008) on top surfaces, and light grey (close to RAL 7044) on undersurfaces. Some had large surfaces (like engine cowlings and the entire fin) painted in trainer yellow (RAL 1032) too. The last two of the serial were usually applied in rudder, most often in white (like here), sometimes in black. Campaign stripes were added to fuselage and wings.

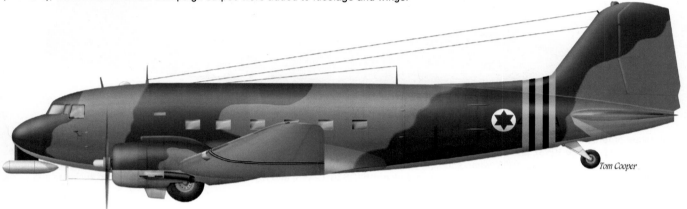

Venerable Dakotas were amongst the first aircraft to participate in the Suez Campaign, carrying paratroopers that attacked Mitla Defile, in central western Sinai. This aircraft – registered as 4X-FAA – was camouflaged in standard brown/blue/light grey scheme (covered by campaign stripes on the rear fuselage), and was equipped with ASH radar, used for maritime patrols in addition to its transport task.

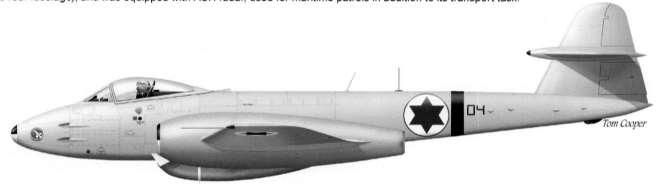

Painted in high speed silver colour overall, Israeli Meteors received 'identification markings' in form of their nose tip and intake lips painted in (clockwise) black-white-black-white, and the vertical fin forward bulb painted in black. Their hooded canopies were replaced by non-hooded versions in late 1955. Instead of campaign stripes, they usually received only one black strip around the rear fuselage.

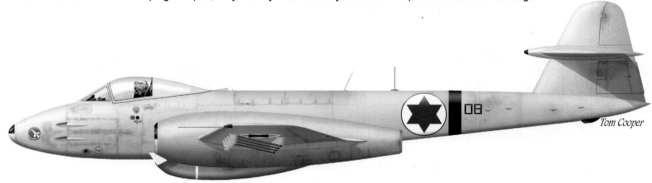

By October 1956, most of 11 Israeli Meteor F.Mk. 8s acquired from Great Britain in 1953 were well-weathered. Notable are launch rails for US-made HVAR unguided rockets, four of which were installed under the wings Notable is application of the unit insignia of the 'First Jet Squadron' on the nose and that this aircraft was one of the few retaining the hooded canopy.

Colour profile commentaries and images by Tom Cooper.

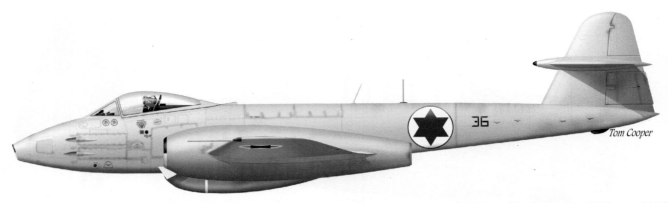

Except for F.Mk. 8s, Israel acquired seven ex-RAF FR.Mk. 9s, refurbished by Flight Refuelling Ltd, in 1954. Left in their original high speed high speed silver colour overall, they are not known to have worn any campaign strips as of October 1956. This example had two kill markings applied underneath the windshield commemorating the downing of two Egyptian Vampires on 1 September 1955.

Although Israel ordered six Meteor NR.Mk. 13 night fighters from Great Britain, only three of these arrived in September and October 1956 (the other three arrived in March 1958), and there was only one crew available for them. This aircraft, serial number 52, fired the opening shots of the campaign on the night of 28 October 1956, when shooting down an Egyptian Air Force Ilyushing Il-14 transport, believed to be carrying members of the Egyptian High Command. The aircraft was painted in dark earth (BS381C/450) and royal sea blue (BS381C/106) on top surfaces and sides, and extra dark sea grey (BS381C/640) on undersurfaces.

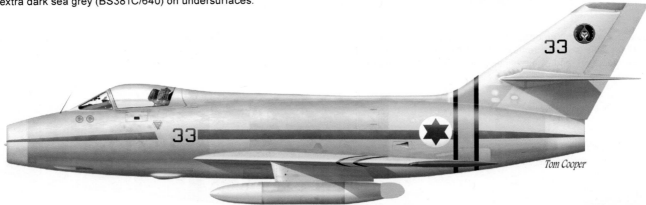

Left in natural metal overall, the Dassault Mystère IVAs of No. 101 'First Fighter' Squadron received a bright red strip down their entire fuselage. During the Suez Campaign of 1956, they received rather incomplete campaign stripes in form of a thick yellow strip outlined in black. Illustrated here is the aircraft with full serial number 4533, the last two of which were applied below the cockpit and on the fin. It received two kill markings for two Vampires claimed as shot down on 1 November 1956.

Belonging to the second batch of Mystère IVAs delivered to Israel, and originally slanted to enter service with another unit, this aircraft (full serial 6684) received very large serials applied in black on the forward fuselage, but also complete campaign stripes. It is shown as in configuration for attack on Ras Nasrani, on 2 November 1956, armed with pods for seven unguided rockets calibre 68mm, when it was shot down by Egyptian AAA. The pilot ejected safely and was recovered by a Piper from No. 100 Squadron, shortly later.

Colour profile commentaries and images by Tom Cooper.

Left in natural metal overall, this Ouragan (full serial 5628) wore no other special markings but campaign stripes (and its wing-tip fuel tanks painted in red) and is thus most representative for the look of majority of about 30 aircraft of this type in service with 'Hornet' Squadron during the Suez Campaign.

The Suez Campaign interrupted the process of camouflaging the Ouragans and thus only a few flew in the standard brown, blue and light grey colours as of October-November 1956. Nevertheless, quite a few have received the sharkmouth insignia on their front fuselage, together with campaign stripes on the rear fuselage and around both wings.

This Ouragan received a full set of 'Hornet' Squadron's insignia, including the unit patch on the top of the fin and the sharkmouth insignia, and a small red 'bolt' on wing-tip fuel tanks. The type was the first French-made jet fighter in Israeli service and proved a stable gun platform, well-suited to attack missions, as well as able to survive some punishment: although seven were damaged in air combats and by ground fire, and at least four made belly-landings, none was written off.

This Ouragan belonged to a batch of aircraft that received slightly different campaign strips, consisting of a wide yellow band, crudely outlined in black. All Israeli aircraft of this type carried roundels in six positions. Except for four cannons calibre 20mm installed internally, their standard armament included four HVAR unguided rockets calibre 68mm, and bombs calibre 250kg (500lbs) bombs.

Colour profile commentaries and images by Tom Cooper.

Operated by No. 116 'Flying Wing' Squadron, this P-51D Mustang (full serial 2304) had its spinner painted in red and went into action without wearing campaign strips. It is shown in standard armament configuration for this war, including six HVAR unguided rockets and two 125kg (250lbs) bombs. Not designed for ground attack, Mustangs suffered heavily from Egyptian ground fire: the pilot of this example was forced to make a belly landing after receiving hits into its oil-filled radiator, on 1 November 1956.

Operated by No. 105 'Scorpion' Squadron (which usually painted spinners of its aircraft in yellow), this is probably one of best-known Mustangs of the Suez Campaign in 1956. Camouflaged in the standard blue and brown camouflage on upper surfaces and sides, with light grey undersides, it received partial campaign strips in form of a wide yellow band, outlined in black, around the rear fuselage and wings, as usual for Mustangs of this squadron. This P-51D was badly damaged by ground fire and forced to make belly landing, on 31 October 1956, its pilot becoming the sole Israeli POW of this war.

Also shot down over the Sinai (on 2 November 1956) was this Mustang operated by No. 116 'Flying Wing' Squadron, serial number 2373. It provided a good example for application of campaign strips by this unit: since they followed the official rules and applied all three bands in yellow and two in black, there was not enough space for all of these on the rear fuselage. Correspondingly, the technicians painted them (crudely and with brush) partially over the national insignia and partially over the serial number.

Colour profile commentaries and images by Tom Cooper.

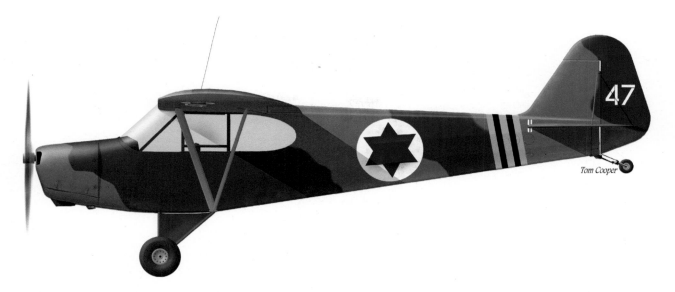

Operated by the 'Flying Camel' Squadron, versatile Piper Cubs were used for liaison, communication, search and rescue, and casualty evacuation during the Suez Campaign. All were painted in standard brown colour overall, some having a camouflage pattern in blue applied on upper surfaces and sides, while undersides were left in grey colour. Most have received campaign stripes – usually applied in rather crude fashion, often covering the serial number (when this was applied on the fuselage) or, like in this case, inclined across the rear fuselage. Two Pipers of No. 100 Squadron were destroyed by Egyptian MiGs during operations near Mitla Defile on 30 October 1956: the aircraft shown here was destroyed on the ground by cannon fire, while another example was shot down and its crew killed.

Colour profile commentaries and images by Tom Cooper.

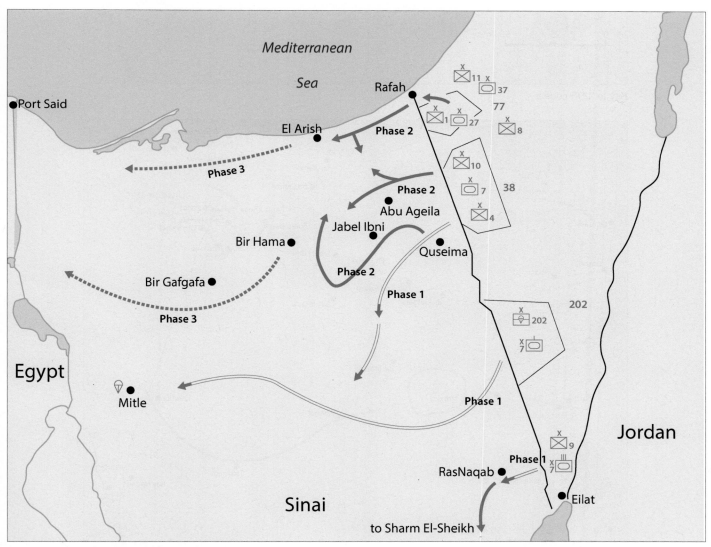

Operation KADESH 2 plan issued on 28 October 1956.

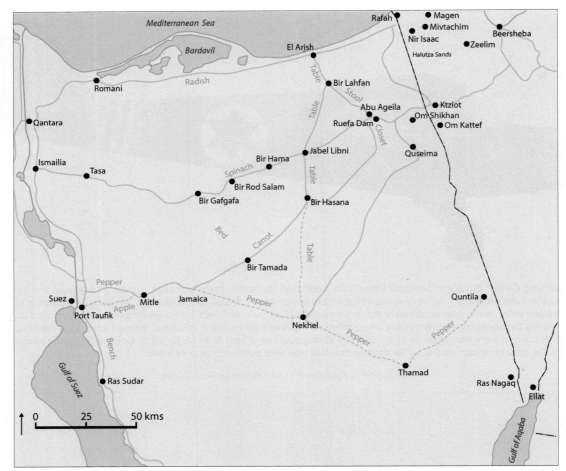

Key to ILDF codes.

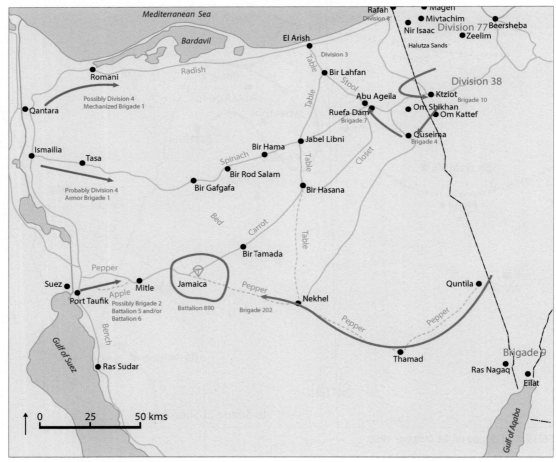

Map showing situation at end of Day 2.

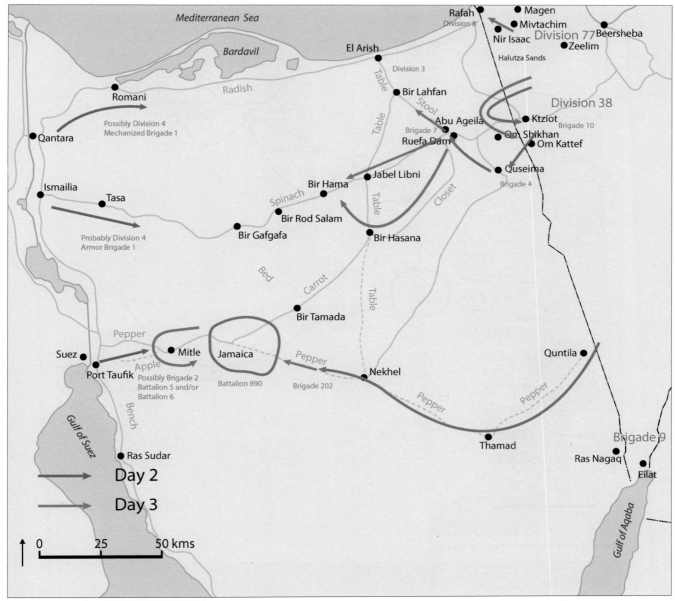

Map showing situation at end of Day 3.

P-51 73 as photographed at the crash site in 1967. For some unknown reason, 2373 was turned upside down some time between 1957 and 1967.

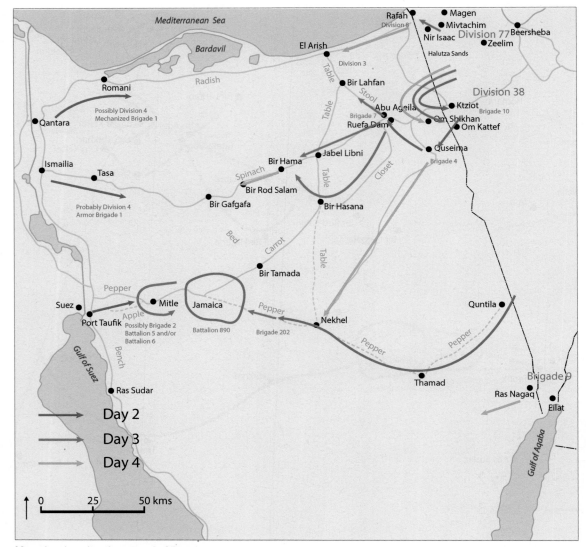

Map showing situation at end of Day 4.

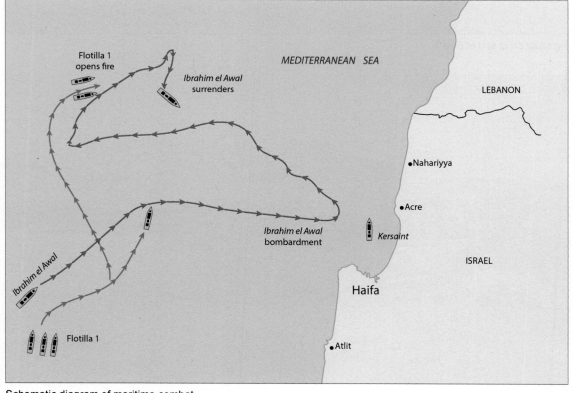

Schematic diagram of maritime combat.

An Egyptian vehicle reportedly hit during an ILAF strike along RADISH between Rafah and El Arish.

The only MiG wreckage pinpointed in Sinai during ILDF post-Suez War occupation and therefore most likely the MiG that Jacob Nevo shot down on 31 October 1956.

Mystère 85 adorned with a kill marking as photographed in May 1958.

Qantara. David Gatmon recalled:

> The [El Arish] airfield was not active [as an air base]... the hangars were used for storage... and we were tasked to bomb [the hangars] ... [bombing] hits were good... and we were then tasked to attack convoys [along RADISH] ... We were [a] four-ship formation and we split into two pairs; I was the leader of the second pair... My wingman was Amram Shemer and my guns jammed after the second or third [strafing] attack so I was unable to shoot any more and I waited for him. I circled overhead to look after him, saw him diving and attacking, and AAA hit me... I told him that I got hit and that I was injured so he stopped attacking, escorted me and helped me to return back home. There was a lot of activity with British and French aircraft in the air and aircraft carriers at sea and a lot of mess in control [radio traffic] so I did not try to land at Tel Nof or at Hatzor; I did not know the codes and dragged myself [all the way] to Ramat David. I was wounded, badly, in my leg and also in my hand; I was losing blood from my leg... I did not feel good... I was very thirsty... I did not know the extent of damage to the aircraft but I made it [to Ramat David] and only later it turned out that a belt, a chain that held controls, was torn and – like in a bicycle [chain and sprockets] – only the upper part held on, the lower part was torn...

METEORS OVER RADISH

1315–1410	117	3606	Kaspit	interdiction RADISH
1315–	117	Meteor	Gat	ditto

IOKR indicated that the two Meteors that took off at 1315 claimed the destruction of eight vehicles and a train. IOKB indicated that two Meteors attacking at 1335 claimed to have destroyed ten vehicles. The two Meteors that took off at 1315 were the only Meteor pair in the air at 1335.

EJECTION FROM MIG

1325–1350	101 yellow1	4560	Gonen	patrol Sinai
1325–1350	101 yellow2	4543	Dekel	ditto
1325–1425	101blue1	4585	Nevo	patrol Sinai
1325–1425	101blue2	4533	Zuk	ditto

Squadron 101's blue section encountered two MiGs over El Arish

and engaged one MiG that the pilots claimed was a MiG-17, possibly because the ILAF figured that the MiG-15 was not equipped with an ejection seat while the MiG-17 had an ejection seat. Jacob Nevo reported:

> While chasing him, I closed range down to 200 yards and he stabilized in my sight. I squeezed trigger; not a long burst. He immediately entered a quick spin. I did not see parts of structure disintegrating even though my round hit its airframe. At 10,000 feet [altitude the aircraft] leveled and the pilot ejected. I saw the ejection seat flying out [of the aircraft] but I did not see that the parachute opened. The MiG-17 [then] descended in flames.

AMV1 identified the EGAF MiG-15 pilot as Fuad Kamal, whose story remarkably overlapped the ILAF narrative in a number of key details.

FROM MITLE PATROL TO MITLE BATTLE

1350–1500	101 khaki1	4529	Lev	patrol Sinai
1350–1500	101 khaki2	4546	Lapidot	ditto

While the ILDF focused attention on the successful offensive of Brigade 7 in the Abu Ageila to Bir Hama section of SPINACH and

Brigade 10's failed attack against the Om Kattef fortifications, reports concerning the Brigade 202 patrol from JAMAICA to Mitle started to filter in. At 1330 the ILDF notified AIR3 that three companies from Brigade 202 – practically the force of a battalion – were patrolling from JAMAICA to Mitle. At 1350, more than an hour after the Brigade 202 patrol started to advance from JAMAICA, Command South notified the ILDF of a patrol in the direction of Mitle. By then, the Brigade 202 patrol was already in contact with EGDF troops defending Mitle, engaged in heavy fighting and suffering from communication troubles to the point that only FAC Mobile Number 24 continued to maintain communication, and even this communication channel was troublesome. The Brigade 202 patrol commander reported to the ILDF via FAC Mobile Number 24 HF radio, the ILDF relayed the patrol commander's messages to Brigade 202 Commander, who transmitted messages to FAC Mobile Number 24 on VHF because of the two FAC Mobile Number 24 VHF radios, one was completely unserviceable and one semi-unserviceable as it was able to receive but not transmit; on top of these communication difficulties, FAC Dov Matos was injured in his hand.

While what was supposed to be a patrol was evolving into a fierce battle, Squadron 101's khaki section attacked along PEPPER west of Mitle. It was practically impossible for ILAF aircraft to support the Brigade 202 patrol around Mitle due to the proximity of EGDF and ILDF troops.

VAMPIRE DUMMIES AGAIN

1400–	113	Ouragan Harlev	interdiction RADISH and/or SPINACH
1400–	113	Ouragan Dan	ditto
1400–	117	Meteor Ben Aaron	attack El Arish airfield
1400	117	Meteor Altman	ditto

Squadron 113 pilots reported a train travelling from Gaza to Khan Yunes and observed the EGDF's Armor Brigade 1 forces along SPINACH between Bir Hama and Bir Gafgafa. Squadron 117 pilots attacked, again, the Vampire dummies at El Arish; AAA fire hit one Meteor with four rounds.

FRIENDLY FIRE INCIDENT AT BIR HASANA

| 1430–1845 | 100 | Piper | Levy | Beer Sheba/Ktziot; CASEVAC Bde 202 |

ILAF operations slowed down and no combat aircraft departed bases from 1400 until 1450; it was then that the impact of the Mitle patrol-turned-battle started to sink in and to draw attention, focus and resources, especially concerning CASEVAC.

The success of Brigade 7 to practically cut the EGDF fortifications at Om Kattef motivated a message to Squadron 103, from around 1405, to prepare a psywar C-47 equipped with loudspeakers; a mission that would be flown much later, after sunset.

The patrol and battle of Brigade 202 prompted preparations for CASEVAC from Mitle. At 1410, Squadron 103 reported a requirement to prepare a C-47 for delivery of blood to forces in Sinai, presumably to Brigade 202. At 1415, Tel Nof ordered Squadron 103 to prepare a C-47 that would transport fuel to JAMAICA and perform CASEVAC on the return flight; Michael Ben-Josef was named to fly this mission.

While occupied with the implications of the Mitle battle, the ILDF also planned ahead and at 1430 ordered Command South to initiate Division 77's offensive in the direction of Rafah during the night of 31 October to 1 November. The ILDF's unplanned preoccupation with the implications of Brigade 202's Mitle battle was emphasized at 1435 when the ILDF indicated that it was in contact with Brigade 202 ALO and that it was planning air support.

Meanwhile – since C-47 CASEVAC was impossible because an airfield for airlifters at JAMAICA had not been prepared yet, and because the ILAF avoided airlift operations over Sinai during daylight until the accomplishment of air superiority, which was not expected before 1 November – a Piper was tasked to fly a CASEVAC mission in support of Brigade 202, to evacuate a casualty from Mitle to Lod. Pilot Reuben Levy reported:

> I departed Beer Sheba and flew along road [CARROT], [flying offset road] some half a mile south of the road, in direction of drop zone [JAMAICA]. At map reference... I saw a P-51 that belly landed. I circled over the aircraft and saw that it was intact, the cockpit was empty, the pilot parachute was on the seat, closed; aircraft number 19 [2319, the P-51 that Eldad Paz had landed around 1410, only about an hour or so before the appearance of Reuben Levy in his Piper!]. I returned to Bir Hasana... [landed] and informed Battalion [9] Deputy Commander [about the P-51]. At the time [more likely sometime later and certainly after 1700] they [Battalion 9] moved north [from Bir Hasana to link-up with Battalion 52 at Bir Hama]. When I was [still] on the ground [at Bir Hasana], and so were our forces [Battalion 9], four Ouragans appeared at around 1700 and attacked; napalm injured a number of our troops, including Battalion [9] Commander. Battalion [9] Deputy Commander told me that our aircraft attacked them, at that place [Bir Hasana], five times: Mosquitoes, Ouragans and possibly P-51s. After the Ouragans attack I took off and flew to Mitle to evacuate casualty but I was unable to find them [Brigade 202 and/or JAMAICA] so I decided to return.

Also reporting a friendly fire air strike was Brigade 7's Battalion 82, that was deployed north of Abu Ageila in direction of El Arish while also engaging the Om Kattef fortifications. Battalion 82 reported an ILAF Meteors attack at 1430. IOKR concluded that this was probably not a 'friendly fire' incident and the attackers were probably EGAF Meteors; this conclusion was based on ILAF timing of Squadron 117 Meteor missions. However, if Battalion 82's timing of this attack was punctual, and if ILAF timing of Squadron 117 Meteor missions was also punctual, then the only ILAF Meteors in the air at 1430 were the pair that reportedly raided El Arish airfield, not far from Battalion 82 deployment.

PATROL OVER P-51

| 1450–1550 | 101 | 4547 | Bar white1 | patrol Sinai |
| 1450–1550 | 101 | 4590 | Bet On white2 | ditto |

Squadron 101's white section patrolled over the downed P-51, presumably 2319 that Piper pilot Reuben Levy pinpointed west of Bir Hasana, but, if so, then at the time the P-51 pilot, Eldad Paz, had

The third and final known attack against Vampire dummies at El Arish was some time after 1400. The dummies were even assigned with realistic EGAF numbers in the same range as real Vampires.

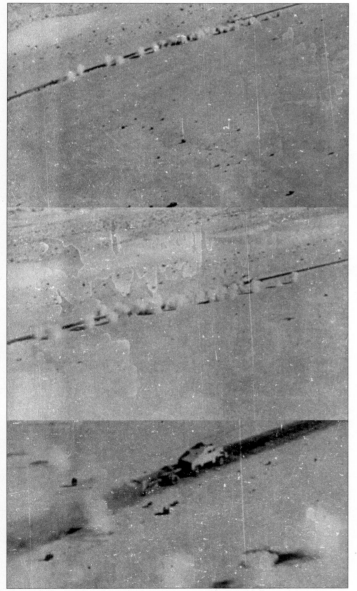

Squadron 117 Meteor pilot Mordehy Lavon reportedly took these sight camera images while strafing an Egyptian vehicle travelling along SPINACH on 31 October 1956. The images could have been taken during Squadron 117 mission from 0835, 1250 or 1500, but if taken along SPINACH and if Lavon did not fly the mission from 1500 then these images were most likely taken during the mission from 0835.

already cleared the area and was hiding in preparation for his night-time walk to Bir Hasana.

FRIENDLY FIRE OVER SPINACH?

1500–1550	117	3735	Zivoni	interdiction SPINACH
1500–1540	117	3603	Sarig	ditto
1500–1550	117	Meteor	Lavon	ditto
1500–1550	117	Meteor	Yahalom	ditto

IOKR indicated that this mission was flown in four-ship formation, listed names of the four pilots as presented above and reported that they hit five vehicles. IOKB stated that two Meteors attacked at 1535 south of Jabel Libni and claimed the destruction of one tank, two half-tracks and one vehicle. Nahum Yahalom reported three sorties on 31 October; had he flown this mission as well, then there should have been four flights. It is therefore possible that only Adam Zivoni and Yossi Sarig actually flew this mission.

Battalion 52 occupied Jabel Libni circa 1400 and started to advance, along SPINACH, from Jabel Libni to Bir Hama at around 1600. It was during Battalion 52's movement from Jabel Libni to Bir Hama that Meteors attacked; the attacking Meteors hit a half-track and a Jeep and injured seven troops; Battalion 52 Commander's opinion was that the attackers were ILAF Meteors.

Again, accurate timing is critical. If all presented timings were punctual, then the Squadron 117 Meteors, four or two, RTBed by 1540 or 1550 while Battalion 52 was attacked some time after 1600. If this was indeed the case, then it is highly likely that the attacking Meteors were Egyptian and not Israelis. On the other hand, AIR4 did not track any EGAF Meteors attack around that time and it is highly likely that all mechanized forces in the Jabel Libni sector, at the time of the Squadron 117 Meteors mission, were Israeli.

ALMOST INTERCEPTION OF RECCE METEORS

1500–1625	115	3518	Livneh/Galon Yud178 photograph south Sinai (Abu Ageila/Bir Hama)
1500–	117	Meteor	Alroy Yud178 escort
1505–1635	115	3517	Eyal/Shchori Yud177 photograph south Sinai (Jabel Libni/Mitle)
1505–	117	Meteor	Gat Yud177 escort

ILDF/I ordered the ILAF to photograph south Sinai at 0400 and at 0855; AIR3 issued MIOR Yud177 at 0715 and MIOR Yud178 at 1030. MIOR Yud177 tasked Squadron 115 to photograph south Sinai in a Squadron 117 Meteor trainer equipped with a 24in camera. MIOR Yud178 tasked Squadron 115 to photograph south Sinai in a Squadron 117 Meteor trainer equipped with a 36in camera. Each of the photographing Meteors was to be escorted by a Squadron 117 pilot, in a Squadron 117 Meteor fighter.

Squadron 115's laboratory handled the MIOR Yud178 film from 1705, processing 100 negatives and producing 300 prints, with first data distributed from 1955 and first prints posted from 2100. The same laboratory handled the MIOR Yud177 film from 1820, processing 71 negatives and producing 213 prints, with first data distributed from 2020 and first prints posted from 2120.

Squadron 115 pilot Meir Livneh, standing in front of a Mosquito, flew MIOR Yud178, in a Meteor, on 31 October 1956.

Squadron 113 servicemen refuel Ouragan 75, painted with ILAF Suez War IFF stripes version 1, probably after return from flight.

IOKR reported that when the two MIOR Yud178 Meteors were over Bir Hama – not exactly in south Sinai – ILAF control identified the Meteors as enemy aircraft and vectored Mysteres to intercept. At this time there were three Mystère pairs in the air: the first – Squadron 101's white section – reportedly patrolled over P-51 not far away from Bir Hama, while the other two pairs operated over the CYPRUS sector. IOKR reported that the Mystère pilots vectored to intercept what ILAF control identified as enemy aircraft, identified the Squadron 115 reconnaissance Meteor and the escorting Squadron 117 Meteor as friendly aircraft and did not attack.

Squadron 115 Commander Eli Eyal, flying MIOR Yud177 at about the same time, recalled, years later, that Mysteres attempted to intercept his section, that he was unable to communicate with the Mystère pilots due to a communication system malfunction and that a 'friendly fire' incident was avoided when Mystère leader Dror Avneri identified the Meteors as Israeli aircraft.

Squadron 117 pilot Hillel Alroy, reportedly flying MIOR Yud178, also recalled, years later, that the mission was to photograph Mitle from 30,000 feet and that, over Mitle, Ouragans saw the Meteors overhead, asked ILAF control if any ILAF Meteors were flying over Mitle, were given a negative answer and then climbed to intercept the Meteors, but a 'friendly fire' incident was avoided when Alroy identified the voice of Ouragan pilot David Ivry.

Obviously, it is possible that both had happened; that Ouragans almost intercepted the MIOR Yud177 Meteors over Mitle and Mysteres nearly engaged the MIOR Yud178 Meteors over Bir Hama.

BRIGADE 202 REQUEST AIR SUPPORT

1520–	113	Ouragan Hod	support Bde 202
1520–	113	Ouragan Furman	ditto
1520–	113	Ouragan Bareket	ditto
1520–	113	Ouragan Rosen	ditto

The ILDF noted, at 1500, a Command South report that a Brigade 202 patrol encountered the enemy some five kilometers west of JAMAICA, was engaged in combat and was requesting air support. At this point, at 1500, there was only one ILAF formation over Sinai – Squadron 101's white section – and the slowdown in operations was exploited for a few reports. At 1510, the ILDF indicated that a Brigade 11 battalion would be ready to move to Tel Nof by 1800; this was probably in connection to the planned airlift to JAMAICA. At 1516, AIR3 reported to the ILDF that the ILAF had shot down, up to that time, six MiGs and four Vampires; the actual claim was probably three MiGs and three Vampires.

The first formation tasked to support Brigade 202 was a Squadron 113 four-ship formation that actually attacked traffic along the route from Mitle to Suez, west of the Brigade 202 battle in the Mitle Pass.

ENGINE CYLINDER BLOCK

1520–1655	116	2303	Yavneh	interdiction SPINACH
1520–	116	P-51	Burstein	ditto
1520–1655	116	2352	Etkes	ditto
1520–	116	P-51	Hativa	ditto

While Squadron 113 Ouragans were assigned to support Brigade 202, ILAF support of the ILDF's main effort during Day 3, Brigade 7's advance from Abu Ageila to Bir Hama, continued with interdiction along SPINACH. The Squadron 116 P-51 pilots attacked a force that was estimated to include some 100 vehicles. IOKB indicated that P-51s attacking at 1600 claimed the destruction of two tanks, one armored car and one half-track. IOKR stated that the Squadron 116 P-51 pilots claimed to have destroyed two tanks, one armored car, one half-track and seven trucks. Squadron 116's narrative indicated that pilots claimed the destruction of one armored car, one half-track, seven trucks and possibly two tanks. Jonathan Etkes reported:

> During final pass, in between Bir Hama and Bir Gafgafa, the left [engine cylinder] block exploded and I returned with severe vibrations; to my credit [destruction of] a communication vehicle and a truck and probable [destruction of] one tank.

SQUADRON 105 COMMANDER KILLED

1525–	105 black1	2336	Tadmor	interdiction SPINACH
1525–1655	105 black2	2331	Niv	ditto
1525–1725	105 black3	2310	Hagani	ditto
1525–1725	105 black4	2339	Bodilewski	ditto

Also tasked to attack the EGDF's Armor Brigade 1 along SPINACH was Squadron 105's black section that departed Ramat David at 1525. Haim Niv recalled:

> We passed over a locality with AAA... I think that we flew too high... maybe even too slow... The lower you fly, the shorter

This photo has been claimed to depict the crashed and burning P-51 2336.

Squadron 105 end-of-war pilots photo; Haim Niv is crouching first from left; Isaiah Bodilewski is standing second from left.

alert for AAA; it was all manual, there was no radar [guidance] so suddenly the [AAA] gunner spotted an aircraft; if the aircraft flew at 30 feet [AGL] then AAA may not have had enough time to react; if the aircraft flew at 200 or 300 feet [AGL] then [AAA] saw the aircraft from [a range] of three to four kilometers and had time for whatever little was needed to aim.

There was AAA [fire] but I did not see that [Moshe] Monik [Tadmor] was hit, not that I did not feel and know that I was hit. Suddenly [Shlomo] Henig [Hagani] yelled 'Number 1, you are pouring black smoke'. I looked and I saw a little bit of black smoke, so why yelling? But Monik started to turn right, we were heading south-west, and Henig said 'I am pressing ahead with Number 4' and I think that he also told me to follow Number 1. Monik did not say a word. From that moment I did not hear him and I did not try to contact him; I figured that if he did answer Henig then he would not answer me. Monik turned and flew, full power, in direction of Israel and I followed him, also in full power. At a certain phase, it is difficult to synchronize events, he jettisoned ordnance, launched rockets... ejected canopy and I saw him flying without canopy but the windshield was all black, from oil, I am always certain it was oil because glycol was not black. By then his engine already stopped, or lost power, because he slowed down and I, still in maximum throttle, overtook him. I was on his right when I overtook him so I turned left and then right, but by the time I finished this simple maneuver that should have taken no more than 10 to 15 seconds... he was already on the ground, burning. The center of the fuselage, cockpit and fuel tanks, burnt in fiery fire. I circled overhead several times and RTBed.

I assumed that I jettisoned ordnance... and I returned home at low altitude, alone, and when I landed it was already getting dark, twilight time. When I landed I sensed a flat tire and the aircraft initiated a swing to the right; I reacted with brakes; the aircraft stopped quite quickly on the runway. Technical Officers, Norik [Harel] and maybe Abraham Kidon, approached my aircraft and I told them 'I think Monik was killed'. Why did I not say 'Monik was killed'? I had two reasons. I was afraid of saying such a terrible statement. I had the slightest doubt that maybe it was not him because I lost him for a moment; maybe someone else crashed during the 10 to 15 seconds that I did not see him... but it was him and the aircraft number was still readable when I visited the crash site about a week later. It turned out that my aircraft was also hit from a lot of small fragments, there were 34 holes, but vital systems were not damaged except for [a] flat tire.

IOKB indicated that four P-51s attacked at 1630 some 14 kilometers west of Bir Hama and claimed the destruction of two tanks; IOKR reported that Squadron 105 black 3 and 4 attacked between Bir Hama and Bir Gafgafa and claimed to have destroyed two tanks; Isaiah Bodilewski reported attack near Bir Gafgafa and hitting one tank and two tracked vehicles.

INTERDICTION MITLE/SUEZ

1530–	113		Ouragan Halivni	support Bde 202
1530–1640	113	4047	Ivry	ditto

Amnon Halivni and David Ivry also attacked along the route from Mitle to Suez; IOKR stated that the four Ouragans that took off at 1520 and the two Ouragans that took off at 1530 claimed the destruction of some 10 vehicles west of Mitle.

FRIENDLY FIRE INCIDENT

1540–	110		Mosquito Somech	
			attack/ interdiction El Arish/Jabel Libni	
			or Jabel Libni/Bir Hama	
1540–1725	110	2169	Proshanski/	ditto
			Dishoni	
1540–	110		Mosquito	Amiran ditto

The three Mosquitoes were scrambled from Ramat David and tasked in the air en route to target. Control claimed that the Mosquitoes were tasked to attack the road between Jabel Libni and Bir Hama; a sector already mostly, if not wholly, in the hands of Brigade 7's Battalion 52. The Mosquito leader reported that the assigned target was to attack the road from El Arish to Jabel Libni that was mostly not in ILDF hands at the time. It is possible that the Mosquitoes attacked neither, because Brigade 7's Battalion 82, deployed at the Abu Ageila sector, reported what appeared to be a Mosquitoes attack. A Battalion 82 tank commander reported:

Sometime after 1630, came two aircraft, each with two engines, that [previously] attacked Om Kattef fortification [east of Abu Ageila and still in EGDF hands]. They bombed [Om Kattef fortification], circled and strafed the fortification from north. One strafed the fortification and the other continued and strafed us; it was then that I was hit. I identified these aircraft as Israeli.

Another Battalion 82 troop provided a contradicting description:

I was standing with a group of persons at the Abu Ageila/ Daika junction when I saw three Mosquitoes overhead. They bombed at a distance of half a kilometer to our west where Brigade [7] HQ was located...

Until then, Brigade 7 operated practically without ALO and/or FAC, since the FAC Mobile Number 10 assigned to Brigade 7 retreated to Quseima for repairs. The Brigade 7 Commander therefore signaled to Quseima to order FAC to signal to aircraft to stop the attack, but the FAC VHF malfunctioned. The Squadron 110 Mosquito leader reported some 20 armored vehicles at Jabel Libni; the Mosquitoes then bombed and strafed until someone – it is not known who, perhaps one of the Mosquito pilots or another ILAF pilot, because the Brigade 7 FAC Mobile Number 10 was reportedly unable to transmit – shouted that they were attacking ILDF. It was then that the Mosquitoes jettisoned their remaining bombs somewhere in the sands, so it is possible that the Battalion 82 tank commander saw the bombing of the Om Kattef fortifications to the east and that the Battalion 82 troop saw the jettisoning of bombs to the west.

EGAF ATTACK BRIGADE 202

1550–1705	101	4543	Avneri	support Brigade 202
1550–1705	101	4535	Gilboa	ditto
1555–1645	101	4564	Alon	support Brigade 202
1555–1645	101	4580	Shadmi	ditto

No Squadron 101 Mysteres were present over Mitle at 1550, when the EGAF attacked Brigade 202, while Ouragans operated west of Mitle. IOKR reported that the EGAF package composed of four attacking Meteors and some six covering MiGs. The Meteors attacked with rockets and strafed, hitting vehicles and mortars. A hit in a vehicle loaded with ammunition caused an explosion that resulted in the burn-out of three more vehicles. Brigade 202's reported casualties toll in this attack was seven killed and 20 wounded. The Ouragans, that were west of Mitle at the time of the EGAF attack, and the Mysteres, that arrived over Mitle a short while after the attack, did not encounter any enemy aircraft.

CASEVAC MITLE?

1610 –	103	C-47	Yaffe	support Bde 202, Tel Nof–JAMAICA –Tel Nof

IOKR claimed that Uri Yaffe commanded a C-47 crew that departed Tel Nof at 1610, tasked to drop supplies to Brigade 202. Upon arrival over JAMAICA, and after Yaffe dropped the supply, IOKR claimed that the Brigade 202 Commander asked Yaffe to land, even though no airfield fit for C-47 aircraft had been prepared yet at JAMAICA, in order to CASEVAC. According to IOKR, Yaffe landed and evacuated to Tel Nof 21 casualties. No other source unearthed thus far supports such a description of events.

At 1620 – ten minutes after Yaffe departed Tel Nof, according

ILAF Mystère reportedly flying over Mitle Pass.

to IOKR – Tel Nof ordered Squadron 103 to prepare for airlift to JAMAICA at a time interval of 15 minutes between aircraft.

At 1630, Tel Nof ordered Squadron 103 to start the airlift to JAMAICA in order to fly a battalion from Tel Nof to JAMAICA and return a Brigade 202 battalion from JAMAICA, thus indicating that the ILDF was not yet aware of the full implications of the Mitle battle that still raged west of JAMAICA, or that these implications did not yet filter down to Tel Nof and Squadron 103. Five minutes later, at 1635, Squadron 103 unfolded a plan for landing at JAMAICA with a FAC in the first aircraft and Runway Unit staff – probably referring to Runway Branch Unit 731 – divided between the following aircraft; the motivation for the plan to airlift Runway Branch Unit 731 to JAMAICA – while Brigade 202 Runway Unit 625 was already at JAMAICA – is not yet known.

MIGS OR MYSTERES?

1635–1710	101 green1	4561	Peled	patrol Sinai
1635–1710	101 green2	4552	Ronen	ditto

Squadron 101's green section engaged six MiGs that attacked ILDF troops in the Abu Ageila sector. Eight more MiGs, possibly tasked to cover the six attacking MiGs, were then noted to approach the combat scene, so the two Mysteres disengaged.

The MiGs reportedly attacked Brigade 7's Battalion 9 that was on the move from Bir Hasana to Bir Hama. Since Battalion 9 had

been attacked before, on several occasions, by ILAF aircraft, the Battalion 9 Commander figured that the attacking aircraft were Mysteres and that this was another 'friendly fire' incident, but it was probably not and the attacking aircraft were, most likely, EGAF MiGs.

Squadron 101 Commander Benjamin Peled engaged MiGs as green 1 on 31 October 1956.

Squadron 113 servicemen arm an Ouragan with rockets during the Suez War. The photo was obviously taken after 0600 on 2 November 1956.

Squadron 103 navigator Abraham Goldreich flew in 1416 to JAMAICA on the evening of Day 3. Goldreich (right) was photographed post-war in an evening dedicated to farewell from French friends who served in Israel during the Suez War. Also attending were Daniel Shapira (left), who was attached to Squadron 101 Mystère during the Suez War, and Battalion 890 Commander Rafael Eitan (right behind the glass Goldreich holds).

SUPPORT BRIGADE 10

1635–	116	P-51	Zeelon	interdiction SPINACH
	116	P-51	Fredilis	ditto
1635–	116	P-51	Geva	ditto
1635–	116	P-51	Kohorn	ditto
1640–	113	4028	Kishon	interdiction SPINACH?
1640–	113	Ouragan	Yariv	ditto
1640–	113	Ouragan	Harlev	ditto
1640–	113	Ouragan	Zahavi	ditto

Until then, Brigade 10 had failed to occupy the Om Kattef fortifications so another Brigade 10 attack was planned to start during evening hours, with Battalion 104 and Battalion 105 to perform a pincer attack against the fortifications. By then, the unplanned Brigade 202 patrol that evolved into the Mitle battle was already diverting ILDF attention, but the ILDF's focus remained on the Division 38 offensive plus preparations for the offensive of Division 77 and control of Brigade 9's movement south.

At 1615, the ILDF noted the occupation of JAPAN and an order to the ILAF to provide maximum possible support, presumably to Division 38 in general and to Brigade 10 in particular. However, it was already late in the day – sunset was at 1654 – and the ILAF was not geared for nighttime support so only two formations attacked at twilight.

The Squadron 116 four-ship formation attacked as a pair; the two wingmen were forced to abort the mission, one before take-off and one after take-off. Arie Fredilis was forced to abort his mission before take-off due to a canopy that did not lock. Number 4 experienced magneto troubles and was forced to jettison ordnance over the Mediterranean Sea and RTB. The leader and sub-leader pressed ahead as a pair. IOKR indicated that they attacked along SPINACH between Bir Hama and Bir Gafgafa and claimed the destruction of one tank, while Egyptian return fire damaged one P-51. Squadron 116's narrative indicated that Arie Zeelon and Shlomo Geva pressed ahead regardless of Squadron 101's green section reports concerning the presence of 14 MiGs over the same sector, and attacked west of AUSTRALIA, hitting a tank with napalm but not strafing due to falling darkness.

The Squadron 113 Ouragans attacked, according to IOKR, a force of some 50 vehicles that was on the move from Bir Hasana to Bir

Hama and claimed the destruction of two tanks. According to IOKB, four Ouragans attacked a camp at Bir Hasana and claimed to have destroyed two tanks. This might have been the attack that Squadron 100 Piper pilot Reuben Levy witnessed while parking at Bir Hasana.

CASEVAC MITLE!

1640–	103	1414	BenJosef/Reubeni/Eyal/Alon Yud165, support Brigade 202, Tel Nof–JAMAICA–TeNof	
1705–2040	103	1420	Biham/Sela/Vronski/Bok support Brigade 202, Tel Nof–JAMAICA–Tel Nof	
17:20	103	C-47	Amrami	ditto
1730–	103	C-47	Ganot	ditto
1740–	103	1418	Ohad/Rom	ditto
1757–	103	Noratlas	Navot	ditto
1810–	103	1416	Shabty/ Ostashinski/Goldreich/ Strasman	ditto
2000–	103	C-47	Bliman	ditto
	103	1405	Kohen/Richter	ditto
	103	1412	Oz/Biran	ditto
	103	1428	Shamir/ Michaeli	Tel Nof–Eilat–Tel Nof
	103	1401	Biran/Vossman	

The first airlifter to land at JAMAICA, in line with data available at the time of writing, was C-47 1414. While Squadron 103 airlifters were on the way to JAMAICA, the ILDF noted, at 1710, a Command South message that Brigade 202 – which normally reported directly to the ILDF during the first phase of Operation KADESH as a task force with a mission unrelated to Command South operations – reported many casualties. At that time, the Mitle battle, that started around 1300, was still raging, so there were no definitive figures concerning casualties; by the end of the Mitle battle, later that evening, the number of Brigade 202 casualties amounted to some 40 killed and around 120 injured; a number of ILDF casualties that was

Squadron 103 Noratlases were ideal for the drop of supplies and only dropped supplies during the the Suez War, while C-47s mostly dropped paratroopers. This photo was taken after 0600 on 2 November 1956 as the aircraft is marked with ILAF Suez War IFF stripes version 2.

Squadron 103 maintainers service a Noratlas - 4X-FAQ or 4X-FAR since 4X-FAP was painted as 4X-ALH during the Suez War - painted with ILAF Suez War IFF stripes version 2 in force from 0600 on 2 November 1956.

ANGLO-FRENCH OFFENSIVE

British and French aircraft initiated an air offensive against EGAF bases – in order to secure air superiority prior to the planned landing of Anglo-French forces at the northern mouth of the Suez Canal and subsequent advance south in order to occupy the entire Suez Canal Zone – initiated at 1830. The best source, thus far available, for details concerning Anglo-French air operations is WOSZ.

PSYWAR OM KATTEF

2125–   103   C-47   Vedeles   psywar Om Kattef

The Anglo-French offensive was expected to ease the ILDF campaign. The EGDF was expected to divert attention and forces to the Suez Canal; the EGAF was expected to be destroyed, with subsequent ILAF air superiority over the battlefield.

The ILDF ordered Division 38, again, at 2030, to attack and occupy the Om Kattef fortifications during the night of 31 October to 1 November. A Squadron 103 C-47 equipped with loudspeakers was tasked to broadcast undermining messages to EGDF troops at the Om Kattef fortifications.

While Brigade 7 armored fists were in nighttime parking, and while Brigade 202 was still focusing on the impact of the Mitle battle, the ILDF noted, at 2100, a position report, at Quntila, from Brigade 9 and then, at 2150, a message from Division 77, that movement from assembly areas had started. The mission of Division 77 was to attack in the direction of Rafah and then El Arish.

ILAF ORDER OF BATTLE

2200–   103   C-47   Vossman support Brigade
                                    202, Tel Nof–JAMAICA
                                    –Tel Nof

AIR1-compiled ILAF order of battle at 2200 on 31 October 1956 was:

most likely higher than in any other single battle during Operation KADESH. As already indicated, Squadron 100 Pipers were able to evacuate about 10 casualties per night. To evacuate from JAMAICA more than 150 casualties, a more radical solution was required and the Squadron 103 airlifters were asked or tasked to land at JAMAICA; among the evacuated casualties that night was Squadron 100 Piper pilot Moshe Bokai, who was treated by the Battalion 890 aid station at JAMAICA since he was injured on the morning of 30 October.

AIR4 INTELLIGENCE REPORT NUMBER 9

        110   2175   Bavli/   reconnaissance
                               Davidson   Syria

Issued at 1745, AIR4 Intelligence Report Number 9 indicated that the ILDF – actually Brigade 7's Battalion 82 – advanced from Abu Ageila to within 10 kilometers of El Arish; other ILDF efforts – Brigade 7's successful advance to Bir Hama, Brigade 10's failed attack against Om Kattef and Brigade 202's controversial patrol that evolved into the Mitle battle – were not explicitly indicated.

The EGDF's main activities – according to AIR4 – were forwarding of reinforcement to the Jabel Libni sector – this was AIR4's reference to the EGDF's Armor Brigade 1 movement from west to east along SPINACH – and a counter-attack in the JAMAICA sector, perhaps an indirect reference to the Mitle battle.

The EGAF's main activities – according to AIR4 – were patrols overhead of reinforcement moving in the direction of Jabel Libni and an attack on ILDF troops at JAMAICA.

AIR4 claimed that EGAF losses amounted to four MiG-15s and three Vampires, plus one Vampire as probable. Actual numbers were, most likely, three MiGs and three Vampires.

Finally, AIR4 indicated that both SYDF and JODF were on alert – and indeed Squadron 110 continued to monitor activity in Jordan and Syria during the night of 31 October to 1 November – while claiming that a JOAF and SYAF attack against Israel was planned for the night of 31 October to 1 November; a doubtful claim since both JOAF and SYAF options for nighttime attack were questionable at best.

Base	Unit	Type	Serviceable for Combat	Serviceable for Flight	Notes
Ramat David	69	B-17	2	-	5 pilots, 4 navigators, 3 radio operators, 19 gunners
	100B	Piper	-	1	2 pilots

Base	Unit	Type	Serviceable for Combat	Serviceable for Flight	Notes
	105	P-51	7	–	7 pilots
	110	Mosquito	not reported	not reported	not reported
	119	Meteor	2 (night fighters)	–	1 pilot, 1 navigator
	199	Mystère	14	–	24 pilots
	201	Mystère	3	3	20 pilots
Dov Field	128	T-17	–	5	not reported
Lod	200	F-84F	9	–	16 pilots
Ramla	100A	Piper	–	4	3 pilots
	147	T-17	–	16	27 pilots
Tel Nof	103	C-47	–	18	28 pilots, 7 co-pilots, 19 navigators,
		Noratlas	–	2	19 radio operators, 1 gunner
	115	Mosquito	3	–	5 pilots, 5 navigators
	116	P-51	11	–	14 pilots
	117	Meteor	6 (including one recce)	2	10 pilots
Hatzor	HQ	T-17	–	2	2 pilots
	101	Mystère	18 (including one recce)	–	22 pilots
	113	Ouragan	20	–	16 pilots
Beer Sheba	100C	Piper	14	–	13 pilots
	140	T-6	15	1	19 pilots
Eilat	100D	Piper	–	5	not reported

The ILAF inventory was obviously larger than the presented figures but this AIR1-assembled ILAF order of battle table was representative of its true strength at the time of preparation and was of utmost importance for AIR3's planning efforts since, for example, it was clear from the table that Squadron 117 was unable to launch more than a four-ship formation until more Meteors would be made serviceable for combat; likewise, Squadron 105's maximum possible effort at that time was a four-ship formation and a three-ship formation. Though ILAF maintainers had all night to improve serviceability rates, AIR3's issue of MIORs had to fit the true potential of the squadrons.

AIR4 INTELLIGENCE REPORT NUMBER 10

Practically ending Day 3, AIR4 Intelligence Report Number 10 was issued at 2359 and covered events up to 2300. In the heading, general section, AIR4 presented the highlights of events from 1700 until 2300:

– Anglo French offensive against military targets in Egypt imitated at 1830...
– Enemy air activity over battlefields increased in comparison with yesterday. MiG aircraft appeared in large formations and supplied efficient cover to ground forces; a few MiG-17s were identified among the [enemy] aircraft.
– Egyptian pilots' handling of MiG aircraft was adequate.
– Opposition of Egyptian ground forces increased; the Egyptians mounted very powerful counter-attacks.

Reference to Egyptian counter-attacks was most likely linked to the Brigade 202 patrol that evolved into the Mitle battle, which AIR4 still

The first thus far unearthed reference to combat loss of an EGAF Meteor was in AIR4 Intelligence Report Number 10, issued at 2359 on 31 October 1956. The exact circumstances of this EGAF Meteor loss are not yet known and it is still possible that this wreckage resulted from a pre-war accident.

conceived as an Egyptian counter-attack.

ILDF activity mentioned was the occupation of Om Kattef, which was incorrect information, and operations in the Abu Ageila and Jabel Libni sectors, but there was no mention of Brigade 202's patrol in the ILDF section as the Mitle battle was still conceived as an Egyptian attack and was thus mentioned in the EGDF activity section.

EGDF activity highlights were the advance of Armor Brigade 1, which was reportedly stopped due to ILAF attacks, and an increase of opposition to the ILDF in the Mitle area; the latter was another indication of how AIR4 – most likely based on ILDF sources – viewed the Mitle battle at the time.

The ILAF's main efforts were interdiction – mostly against Armor Brigade 1 – and air superiority through patrols and combats, as well as the airlift to JAMAICA. In the latter context, AIR4 indicated that 120 casualties were sustained in an enemy attack at the Mitle Pass to JAMAICA sector; the actual number of casualties – not known at the time – was around 160 and the battle – not realized at the time – resulted from the Brigade 202 patrol and not from an EGDF attack.

AIR4's estimate of EGAF losses was four Vampires, two MiGs and one Meteor, with the probability that two or three more MiGs were also lost; it is believed, based on currently available data, that actual losses at that time were three MiGs and three Vampires, while the circumstances of the EGAF Meteor combat loss claim are not yet known.

The EGDF's estimated losses amounted to 30 tanks, 25 armored vehicles and 80 to 90 other vehicles; it is assumed that these figures were cumulative claims based on ILAF debrief reports. The AIR4 Intelligence Report Number 9 claim that a JOAF and SYAF attack against Israel was planned for the night of 31 October to 1 November was not repeated in AIR4 Intelligence Report Number 10.

Day 4
1 NOVEMBER 1956

The ILDF's plans for Day 4 were – the same as for Day 3 – to continue Division 38's attack in the center sector, initiate Division 77's offensive in the north sector and continue Brigade 9's advance in direction of Sharm El Sheikh; as indicated, the Anglo-French attack was expected to ease the ILDF's advance and to secure ILAF air superiority over Sinai.

Command South issued two orders that slightly altered ILDF plans for Day 4. At 0030, Command South assigned Brigade 37 to Division 38 so that Brigade 37 would attack the Om Kattef fortifications. At 0059, Command South ordered Brigade 4 to replace Brigade 202 at Thamad and Nekhel.

IL-28 BOMBING

| 119 | 3852 | Tsiddon/ scramble |
| | | Brosh to intercept |

Regardless of the Anglo-French air raids, EGDF Il-28s – ILAF radars produced several tracks that night – attacked again. Only one bombing has been pinpointed when an aircraft bombed kibbutz Gezer at 0115. The post-war MAT5 report elaborated:

In light of stories of kibbutz Gezer residents, it appears that an aircraft approached, illuminated area and immediately afterwards a loud explosion was heard; one of the residents was sure that it was a jet aircraft. The aircraft dropped a stick of 11 bombs. One of the bombs hit a garage where several tractors were parked. The other bombs fell between buildings around the garage. As a result of [the] explosion, the garage, including equipment inside, was completely wrecked. It appears that fuel inside [the] tanks of tractors ignited and caused a fire. The bombs that exploded in between buildings did not cause a lot of damage. Fragments only destroyed a few aluminum tin walls and disconnected telephone lines. The dispersal of the bombs was within a radius of approximately 20 meters. Depth of craters caused by hits was 60 to 75 centimeters and diameter of craters [was] 120 centimeters... Diameter and depth of craters indicate light bombs, up to 100 kilograms. Parts of tails indicate that the bombs were made in USSR. Dispersal [of bombs] indicates that bombs were dropped in single stick. It is reasonable to assume that bombing was carried out by Ilyushin jet aircraft... It can be assumed, based on stories of a few residents, that the aircraft arrived from west... After bombing, they probably flew east in [the] direction of Jordan.

ILLUMINATION IN VAIN?

| 0130–0250 | 140 | 1128 | Gideoni support FRNF |
| | | | ILNF, illumination |

Division 77 ALO Leslie David Easterman requested extensive air support for attack in the direction of Rafah and the ILDF prepared a support that included FRNF and ILNF bombardments, as well as ILAF bombings.

Squadron 140 was tasked to illuminate in support of the FRNF and ILNF bombardment from 0200. Yossi Gideoni recalled:

The T-6 has eight racks and it was not a problem to fly with eight flares; the flares produced more drag [than bombs] but were lighter [than bombs]. I specialized in adjustments [of flares]: the flare had a safety cable and when it was dropped the cable was disconnected and the timer started ticking, after preset timeframe the flare activated, the parachute deployed and the flare was ignited. [Pre-war] I flew illumination test flights over Ramla and I was well-versed in illumination.

Squadron 140 pilots. Squadron 140 Commander Ovadia Nachman is second from left; Yossi Gideoni is in center in front of right door.

Squadron 140 T-6 with racks for bombs or flares.

I was woken up at midnight and was told ILNF would bombard Rafah camps at 0130 and that I was tasked to illuminate. I realized that due to timeframe required to learn map and adjust flares, I would not make it by 0130. Darkness, blackout, and I flew to Rafah, with eight flares, relying on heading and time. I was briefed to drop flares at 4,000 feet so I flew at 4,000 feet and it was cloudy and I did not know where I was. I saw a hole in the clouds, I figured it was roughly the place so I dropped two flares [to pinpoint location]. I was over Rafah town but I also saw Rafah camps and it was almost 0200. I dropped two flares over [Rafah] camps; AAA fire opened and I escaped in clouds. I waited until the flares were about to be out, returned for a second run and dropped another pair of flares. I repeated this drill with the last pair of flares and disengaged. Throughout this time there was no sign of ILNF [bombardment].

I called Teman Field [so that runway lights would be switched on] but was not answered so I headed to Beer Sheba. I did not see Beer Sheba, [due to] blackout, but I saw braking lights of vehicles and realized that I was over road from Beer Sheba south. I turned back, followed road, saw Beer Sheba and flew back [to Teman Field] at 1,500 to 1,800 feet, which is less than 1,000 feet AGL. I called Teman Field again, this time they heard me and ignited two goosenecks at the start of the runway and one gooseneck at the end of the runway, and I landed.

B-17 23 was the lead ship during Squadron 69's first Suez War mission on 1 November 1956 in support of the Division 77 attack against Rafah. Photographed in a pen at Ramat David during the Suez War, 1623 had been equipped, pre-war, with AN/APS-4 radar for maritime patrol.

additional 90 minutes to two hours timeframe is required for briefing, pre-flight preparations, start-up and taxi. Total timeframe can be halved if squadron would receive routes to target, in which case we can take-off within one hour from acceptance of order.

Also delaying departure and complicating preparations was the AIR3 directive that defined routes over 'no fly' zones; an issue that was cleared up in a telephone conversation. Since support for Division 77 was pre-planned, the bombers were not in contact with Division 77 ALO Leslie David Easterman or Brigade 1 FAC Enoch Vishlitzki – in FAC Mobile Number 20 – or with Brigade 27 FACs: Shlomo Yarkoni in FAC Mobile Number 13 – radio call sign BENCH – and Saul Kilion, who joined Battalion 277. The bombers were in radio contact with ILAF Central Control Unit at Ramla. Possibly for this reason, no attempt was made to mark the target for bombers with searchlights or with artillery illumination.

The two bombers arrived, at 0300, flying from land to sea but were unable to pinpoint target due to darkness and haze. The pair returned for a second lower run, flying at 3,500 feet from north to south, from Mediterranean Sea inland to Sinai. Rafah was identified and the navigators/bombardiers triggered the release of the load but not a single bomb fell away. At the last moment, Central Control Unit ordered not to bomb due to the inability to positively identify the whereabouts of Brigade 27 troops, so the pilots switched off the bombing master switch that overrode the navigators/bombardiers.

The B-17s suggested a third run, but Central Control Unit did not grant permission and bombs were jettisoned over the Mediterranean Sea at 0445. Squadron 69 Commander Jacob Ben-Haim concluded:

IOKR claimed that Gideoni illuminated as planned but the start of the bombardment was rescheduled to 0300 without prior notice to the ILAF, so Squadron 140's illumination was in vain.

ILNF post-war research stated that FRNF cruiser George Leygues, escorted by ILNF destroyers, fired some 150 shells between 0200 and 0230 and that illumination was not in vain:

> Weather was not fair due to low clouds over target; the aircraft managed to accomplish mission and marked target; since naval force pinpointed target prior to aircraft action... the [naval] force did not actually exploit this marking [by the aircraft].

BOMBING RAFAH

0200–	69	1623	Ben Haim/ (Toyster)
			Yud180, support Division 77
0200–	69	1622	Efrat/Josefon ditto
0220 –	103	1430	Ben Josef/Reubeni/Eyal/Alon
			Yud165 Tel Nof–JAMAICA–Tel Nof
0220 –	103	C-47	Gil support
			Bde 202

Squadron 69 B-17s last bombed Rafah on 7 January 1949; the 7 January 1949 mission was flown by 1601 and 1603, which became 1621 and 1623 by October 1956. The third B-17 – 1602 in 1949 and 1622 in 1956 – last bombed Rafah on 3 January 1949. The bombers were the same aircraft, the crews were not. AIR3 issued MIOR Yud180 at 1645 on 31 October, tasking Squadron 69 to bomb Rafah in support of Brigade 27, with TOT at 1800; a timeframe from MIOR issue to TOT that Squadron 69 considered as unrealistic. Squadron 69 Commander Jacob Ben-Haim reported:

> It is our experience that standard timeframe for preparations and departure, up to take-off, is 90 minutes to two hours if the aircraft were already armed. Learning target, details of defending AAA, topography and flight plan can take 90 minutes to two hours. An

> We were only notified that our troops were very close to targets so we could only bomb if we had positive identification of target. Darkness and haze over target made this positive identification very difficult, but if we had known that our troops were west of the fire line (we clearly saw the front line by tracking down the sources of light arms fire) we could have bombed using distance and time method. The fact that we were not in contact with FAC prevented realtime discussion of this issue.

ILLUMINATORS AND BOMBERS

0225–	140	1129	Nachman support Div 77
0225–	140	T-6	Hefer ditto
0230–	140	T-6	Bar Lev support Div 77
			OR Kashpitzki
0230–	140	T-6	Kashpitzki ditto
			OR Moshkovic

Squadron 140 was also tasked to bomb Rafah and dispatched two pairs that departed Teman Field after the Squadron 69 B-17s had

Squadron 140 pilots. Isaac Hefer is standing first from right.

departed Ramat David, and arrived over the target sooner than the B-17s; the T-6s were reportedly over Rafah from 0245. Each pair composed an illuminator with eight flares and a bomber with 50 kilograms bombs. Division 77's Leslie David Easterman reported:

> The T-6s dropped bombs one at a time and the nearest bombs fell some two to three kilometers north of Mivtachim, where was Division 77 HQ... I stopped bombing through use of FAC Mobile.

Brigade 1 also reported that bombs fell in the vicinity of Battalion 13 but no damage or casualties were reported. Ovadia Nachman recalled:

> The night was hazy and dark. The first pair illuminator entered vertigo after take-off; he managed to revert to instruments flying but was lost. I, the bomber, waited for the second pair illuminator. I identified target, bombed and the second pair bomber followed.
> After I landed, it turned out that the pilot who recovered from vertigo and the second bomber were unable to pinpoint the airfield due to blackout and haziness... I told [the pilot of the second bomber] to switch on landing lights and turn. He did so, I saw him and guided him to land. I tried to repeat this with the other pilot but he was farther so I did not see his landing lights. I then told him to drop a flare, saw the flare and gave him an estimated heading to base. A few minutes later, his landing lights were not seen yet so I ordered him to drop another flare and from then on I guided him for safe landing. It later

turned out that one of the flares fell nearby Division [77] HQ at Mivtachim; they figured that ILAF was attacking them in error and called [on the radio] to stop bombing, a bombing that had ended long before.

PSYWAR RAFAH AND SUPPLY NEKHEL

	103	C-47		support Div 77, psywar

Division 38's attack against the Om Kattef fortifications failed again – the ILDF noted, at 0315, a message from Brigade 10 that the attack failed and, at 0400, a message from Division 38 that Brigade 37's attack failed – so Squadron 103's psywar mission in support of Division 38 did not contribute to success, a fact that was not known by the time the psywar C-47 was tasked to support Division 77. At 0330, Tel Nof reported:

> A C-47 with loudspeakers had departed for propaganda over Rafah sector.

Ten minutes later, at 0340, Tel Nof summed up the second wave of airlift support to Brigade 202 during the night of Day 3 to 4:

> Eleven C-47s and six Squadron 203 Nords had taken off to supply equipment to paratroopers at Nekhel.

SUPPORT BATTALION 11

0530–	140	T-6	Lapid	support Div 77
0530–	140	T-6	Peled	ditto
0530–	140	T-6	Ophee	ditto
0530–	140	1156	Peleg	ditto

The first formation assigned to support Division 77 was in contact with Brigade 27 FAC, but supported Brigade 1's Battalion 11. The T-6s were tasked to attack, with rockets, an EGDF fort that was already half in the hands of Battalion 11. IOKR reported that the first pair attacked Egyptian troops, Number 3 attacked Israeli troops but without causing casualties and Number 4 practically belly landed during the low altitude run in to target; the pilot exited the cockpit and linked up with ILDF troops.

DAY 4 DAWN

0540–	200	F-84		interdiction Sinai
0600–1500	100	Piper	Ezekiel/ scout	Ktziot–Ktziot

Squadron 200 dispatched seven four-ship formations of FRAF F-84Fs from 0540 until 1635, on 1 November 1956, for interdiction along RADISH and SPINACH.

105	2324	Bodilewski	Haifa–Ramat-David
105	2328	Dagan	Hatzor–Ramat David
105	2729	Magen	Ramat David–Ramla–Ramat David
110	2170	Orli	test
115	1182	Tavor/Sivron	test
115	2139	Tavor	test
117	3606	Yahalom Kaf6	reconnaissance Jordan

IOKR indicated that Squadron 200 dispatched seven four-ship formations from 0540 until 1635 for interdiction along RADISH and SPINACH. While the first formation of FRAF F-84Fs was en route to Sinai, ILDF/I issued Daily Intelligence Report Number 3 that spread ILDF understandings of EGDF actions:

– Division 4 advanced along SPINACH (Division 4 HQ and Armor Brigade 1) and along RADISH (Mechanized Brigade 1) with objective to link-up with Brigade 6 at the Abu Ageila/Om Kattef sector and to push back the ILDF from Sinai.
– Brigade 2 was tasked to attack the ILDF airhead east of Mitle.

ILDF/I also presented an estimate of enemy losses that included five MiGs, four Vampires, a Meteor and possible loss of three more MiGs; one Vampire pilot was taken prisoner. Again, true numbers at that time were probably three MiGs and three Vampires.

RECCE EGDF ARMOR BRIGADE 1

0640 –	117	3735	Zivoni	reconnaissance Sinai
0640 –0740	117	3731	Sarig	ditto

AIR3 MIOR Kaf7, issued at 0340, tasked Squadron 101 to recce Sinai, at 0615, in order to pinpoint the deployment of the EGDF's Armor Brigade 1; actually Command South, at 0400, reported that interpretation of photos, most likely taken on 31 October, pinpointed Armor Brigade 1 – perhaps the vanguard – at Bir Rod Salam, along SPINACH, west of Bir Hama where Brigade 7's Battalion 9 and Battalion 52 parked.

The two Mysteres were tasked to fly to and from the recce route at 30,000 feet, to fly recce at 5,000 feet and report immediately any significant sightings. However, Squadron 101 did not fly Kaf7 on the morning of 1 November and actually flew only four sorties during Day 4; the low level of activity of Squadron 101 may have been linked to the Anglo-French offensive and operations of FRAF F-84Fs and Mysteres over Sinai.

A pair that did fly recce over Sinai on the morning of Day 4 was from Squadron 117. Tel Nof noted, at 0625, that two Squadron 117 Meteors had already departed to recce SPINACH between Bir Hama and Bir Gafgafa while IOKR indicated that the pair took off at 0640. Either way, on the way back from SPINACH, the pair heard a Division 77 FAC asking for air support so they volunteered and strafed in the Rafah sector.

ILAF Suez War IFF stripes version 2 was somewhat of a variation of version 1, but the most interesting point is that version 2 - although ordered on the morning of 1 November 1956 - was only in force from the morning of 2 November 1956.

At about that time, the FRAF – most likely F-84Fs – attacked along SPINACH; the ILDF noted, at 0645, a message that the FRAF attacked a large convoy, some 100 vehicles, west of Bir Gafgafa with many destroyed; IOKB indicated that a formation that attacked along SPINACH at 0650 – most likely FRAF F-84Fs – claimed the destruction of 15 vehicles.

SINAI STRIPES VERSION 2

ILAF IFF stripes were similar but not identical to Anglo-French IFF stripes, possibly to conceal collusion. It would have been logical for the ILAF to change the version of IFF stripes immediately after the start of the Anglo-French offensive at 1830 on 31 October, but this did not happen and it took a timeframe of some 36 hours for the ILAF to update its IFF stripes; the order was issued some 12 hours after start of the Anglo-French offensive, while implementation was to be in force within roughly 24 hours from order.

MAT3 issued an order at 0645 but available documentation indicates that the order was only distributed at 2105; either way, MAT3 specified a new version of identification stripes:

From 0600 [on 2 November] all aircraft, repeat all aircraft, will carry tactical marking as follow: five tight stripes, each ten centimeters wide, in the colors yellow–black–yellow–black–yellow. This marking will replace the current tactical marking.

STICK THEM UP!

0715–	116 black1	2332	Barak	support Div 77
0715–	116black2	P-51	Bloch	ditto
0715–	116black3	P-51	Hasson	ditto
0715–	116black4	P-51	Naveh	ditto

EGDF resistance at Rafah was stiff. The ILDF noted, at 0650, a request for support that was immediately approved and four P-51s were assigned to support Division 77. Meanwhile, IOKB reported that FRAF F-84Fs attacked Rafah camps at 0710. Squadron 116's black section was scrambled to support Brigade 27 and black leader contacted FAC, but target allocation took some time. Dan Barak recalled:

> I ordered line astern as it was much easier to watch one another. We were getting a lot of AAA fire [so I transmitted] 'if you do not tell me what is happening we will all be shot down, it is ridiculous', he said 'wait, wait, I am looking at my map... do not drop napalm, do not use your rockets, report what you see'.

At the time flying as black 2, Amnon Bloch recalled:

> We flew over [the Gaza] Strip...... at 2,000 feet, loaded with napalm, 220 [mph] and it felt like a dead duck. We were up in the sky and they were down below shooting. Suddenly I saw a fine line emanating from the belly [of P-51 black 1]. I called him '[Dan] Harry [Barak]' – we switched to names because there was a terrible mess [over communication channel] – 'go home, you are losing glycol!'.

Black 1 turned back and headed for home but did not make it. Dan Barak recalled:

> I was very low, 200 to 300 feet, and I was hit. I pulled the aircraft up as far as I could, it was not very high; I jettisoned the hood; I did not have enough time to jettison rockets [so] I landed on the rockets, they were not plugged in, they did not blow, fortunately... I was afraid that the aircraft would explode [so I got further away] but it did not explode so I returned to the aircraft and dismantled the [radio] crystals.
> We all had cowboy pistols; the Egyptians are on this side; the Israelis are going to attack and I am in the bloody middle. It was six in the morning and I waited for three or four hours and then a Jeep came with a guy with a tembel hat. I pointed my pistol and said 'stick them up!'. He retorted 'are you out of your mind? I am from kibbutz Orim; I have been looking for you for hours...'.

The other pilots pressed ahead with the mission and claimed the destruction of one tank, three trucks and two vehicles.

RAFAH JUNCTION OCCUPATION

0740–0855	116	2311	Yavneh	support Div 77
0740–	116	P-51	Burstein	ditto
0740–0925	116	2338	Etkes	ditto
0740–	116	P-51	Hativa	ditto

Scrambled as a four-ship formation, FAC requested the leader to split the formation into two pairs. The first pair was tasked to attack vehicles between Rafah and El Arish and reported the destruction of a trucked vehicle, two trucks, two artillery tow vehicles and a tanker. Both pair leaders reported difficulties in communication with FAC. The second pair was initially tasked to attack an EGDF fortification but due to difficulties in communication was retasked to attack along the road from Rafah to El Arish. Jonathan Etkes reported:

> The Egyptians retreated from Rafah to El Arish in a long column along the road and I was credited [with destruction of] two trucks... a water tanker, a tow vehicle with... gun and probable [destruction of] an armored vehicle.

The ILAF reported to the ILDF, at 0815, that Rafah Junction had been occupied – this information was probably streamed in FAC communication channels – and, at 0900, Command South confirmed that Rafah Junction had been occupied.

BLUE OVER RADISH

0825–1015	105blue1	P-51	Hagani	support Div 77
0825–1015	105blue2	P-51	Magen	ditto
0825–1010	105blue3	P-51	Shaked	ditto
0825–1020	105blue4	2369	Ben Nun	ditto

Squadron 105s blue section noted ILDF troops at Rafah Junction and attacked – with napalm, rockets and guns – along the road from Rafah to El Arish; IOKR indicated that blue claimed the destruction of two tracked vehicles, two towed artillery guns and seven trucks.

BLUE OVER BED

0950–1115	101blue1	4547	Nevo	interdiction BED
0950–1115	101blue2	4535	Zuk	ditto
0950–1115	101blue3	4561	Egozi	ditto
0950–1115	101blue4	4544	Lapidot	ditto

The ILAF slowed down operations over Sinai as FRAF F-84Fs and Mysteres took over. IOKB reported FRAF attacks at 0740, 0800 and 0828. The ILDF noted, at 0855, a Brigade 202 request for air support, with a reply that the FRAF would provide support and a note that expected difficulties in communication between FRAF pilots and ILAF FAC. At 0900, the ILDF noted a report from Brigade 7 that Battalion 52 encountered enemy T-34 tanks at Bir Rod Salam, that fire was exchanged and the enemy was retreating. At 0920, the ILDF noted FAC Mobile Number 22's request for additional attacks along RADISH, east of El Arish. At 0930, the ILDF was notified that the EGDF's Armor Brigade 1 was identified at Bir Gafgafa as well as along BED. This information rang an alarm as BED linked SPINACH to CARROT and it was feared that elements of Armor Brigade 1 were trying to move along BED and CARROT in order to attack Brigade 202, which was practically helpless against armor. This analysis prompted Squadron 101's only mission during Day 4, an interdiction along BED in order to stop Armor Brigade 1's alleged advance in direction of Brigade 202.

BETWEEN BELGIUM AND BULGARIA

1020–1200	110	2168	Levin/Hy	interdiction RADISH
1020–1200	110	2173	Proshanski	ditto
1020–	110	2175	Ash/Segal	ditto
1020–	110	Mosquito	Eyal	ditto

IOKR indicated that the Mosquitoes claimed the destruction of 10 vehicles and to have hit one tank while attacking along RADISH

A Squadron 110 Mosquito at Ramat David during the Suez War. This image was taken after 0600 on 2 November 1956 as the aircraft is marked with ILAF Suez War IFF stripes version 2.

some ten kilometers east of El Arish. IOKB listed two formations as attacking along RADISH, in the El Arish sector, with one formation claiming to have destroyed nine vehicles and the other formation claiming one tank and 11 vehicles; this was probably some kind of duplication. Ramat David's GLO reported:

> Four Mosquitoes over target at 1048 between BELGIUM [west of El Arish] and BULGARIA [east of El Arish]. No worthwhile targets for air attack. Scattered traffic in both directions. Our forces hit eight trucks and one communication vehicle. Antennas were sighted in a small valley east of BELGIUM... Fiery... AAA fire from ElArish...

AAA damaged the first pair of Mosquitoes; both RTBed but the damage to 2173 was subsequently classified as CAT4.

SUPPORT CHINA

1020–	116	P-51	Zeelon	support Div 38
1020–1220	116	2337	Fredilis	ditto
1020–1100	116	2304	Cohen	ditto
1020–	116	2370	Sharon	ditto
1045–1110	116	2351	Geva	support Div 38
1045–	116	P-51	Kohorn	ditto
1045–	116	P-51	Hasson	ditto
1045–	116	P-51	Naveh	ditto

CHINA proved a hard nut to crack. Brigade 10's attacks failed and, in the wake of Brigade 37's attack failure, the EGDF counter-attacked from 0900. The four P-51s flew an IFF pass and it was then that 2304 was hit and Cheetah Cohen was forced to belly land; Cohen walked in the direction of the ILDF lines and linked-up with Brigade 37 troops.

The three P-51s pressed ahead with the mission and were replaced by a four-ship formation that also lost a P-51 to AAA fire; Shlomo Geva landed in between EGDF and ILDF lines. Brigade 10 FAC Dan Hadani reported:

> I immediately called the other aircraft to find out where he landed. I was answered that he landed between our forces and enemy fortifications. I asked them to mark his position by diving over him and I moved to the front line in a command car with a driver and a radio operator. A tanks platoon stopped me at the front line [and] from there I saw the aircraft in between us

and Egyptian fortifications at a distance of one kilometer or so. I asked the local commander to cover me with a tank in order to rescue the pilot [who] I identified, with my binoculars, lying nearby the aircraft. The answer was that nobody was allowed to advance. I decided to go by myself; the radio operator and a tanker volunteered to escort me and to cover me with rifles. I ordered the driver [of the command car] to advance [as much as possible] without revealing [the vehicle to the enemy]; I ordered the aircraft to dive in direction of fortification in case of shootings and we departed to the aircraft. We arrived at the spot in a run. I was acquainted with the pilot, Shlomo Geva, who drew a pistol. I called his name so that he would know me and would not open fire. I realized that he was in a pretty good shape and able to walk, so we withdrew immediately. We ran to the commandcar and on our way back, nearby the front line, a Piper landed and suggested to evacuate the pilot, but I declined as he was injured in his head and forehead so I evacuated him to the medical station.

AAA fire also damaged the P-51s of Hasson and Naveh; IOKR indicated that the P-51s claimed the destruction of an armored vehicle, a tracked vehicle and seven vehicles; a claim that was more typical of an interdiction mission than a support mission.

AIR4 INTELLIGENCE REPORT NUMBER 12

1100–12:25	100A	0490	Shoef/ scout	patrol Command Center

Issued at 1115, AIR4 Intelligence Report Number 12 elaborated upon the impact of the Anglo-French attack:

> Anglo-French air forces attacked, during night and morning, Egyptian airfields along [the Suez] Canal and severely damaged hangars and infrastructure; huge fires were observed all along [the Suez] Canal... Enemy aircraft were not encountered during morning hours; it is reasonable to assume that Anglo-French bombings substantially scaled down the operational potential of EGAF. EGDF units in Sinai are retreating in direction of [the Suez] Canal... Our forces occupied Rafah camps... Along SPINACH our forces are 10 kilometers west of Bir Hama... A reconnaissance flown this

ILAF interdiction impact is evident in this post-war photo taken along a road in Sinai.

morning revealed that hangars and buildings at the center of Fayid airfield were severely damaged; some hangars were burning, other buildings were destroyed. At Abu Sueir, MiGs dispersed in sands were observed. MiG and Il-28 aircraft are concentrated at Almaza airfield... it is not known yet if this redeployment is aimed against our forces or against Anglo-French forces.

INTERDICTION SPINACH

1145–	113	Ouragan Hod		interdiction SPINACH
1145–	113	Ouragan Halivni		ditto
1145–1245	113	4070	Ivry	ditto

A force with some 20 tanks was pinpointed some 10 kilometers south of Bir Gafgafa and attacked with napalm and guns. IOKR indicated the claimed destruction of one tank and three half-tracks as well as a HQ tent; the same source revealed the possibility of a 'friendly fire' incident due to a claim that half-tracks – supposedly not in EGDF service – were destroyed. This possibility was highly unlikely because only at 2000 did the ILDF note a message from Brigade 7 that Battalion 52 was approaching Bir Gafgafa.

IOKB stated that Ouragans attacking south of Bir Gafgafa at 1205 claimed the destruction of one tank, three half-tracks and three self-propelled guns.

SUPPORT DIVISION 38

1155–	117	Meteor	Ben Aaron	support Division 38
1155–	117	Meteor	Alroy	ditto

AAA fire hit the Meteors, both RTBed, and the leader performed SEL. IOKB stated that two Meteors, attacking between Abu Ageila and Bir Lahfan – a sector supposedly in ILDF hands, at least partially – claimed one tracked vehicle and two vehicles.

INTERDICTION SPINACH

1200–1255	113	4051	Agassi	interdiction SPINACH
1200–	113	Ouragan Furman		ditto
1200–1255	113	4044	Sheffer	ditto
1200–	113	Ouragan Erez		ditto

The four Ouragans attacked nearby Bir Gafgafa; IOKR indicated the claimed destruction of one tank, three tracked vehicles and a fuel tanker; IOKB stated that Ouragans attacking Bir Gafgafa at 1220 claimed one tank, three tracked vehicles and one vehicle.

SUPPORT BRIGADE 27

1225–	113	Ouragan Bareket	support Bde 27
1225–	113	Ouragan Lidor	ditto
1225–	113	Ouragan Rosen	ditto
1225–	113	4047	Kishon	ditto

Brigade 27's Battalion 19 encountered, at 1200, enemy fortification BULGARIA, a few kilometers east of El Arish, that stopped the advance along RADISH from Rafah to El Arish. Air support was called but Squadron 113 pilots were unable to IFF and did not attack.

CASEVAC REQUEST

The ILDF noted, at 1230, a request to dispatch a helicopter and Piper to evacuate Brigade 37 Commander Samuel Galinka, who was fatally wounded.

SUPPORT BRIGADE 27

1230–	117	Meteor	Yoeli	support Bde 27
1230–1330	117	3606	Kaspit	ditto

IOKR indicated that the Meteors attacked with unclear results. IOKB stated that aircraft attacking along RADISH between Rafah and El Arish, at 1300 or so, claimed one tank and one truck. Mati Kaspit reported that the pair strafed an Egyptian fortification near El Arish, most likely BULGARIA.

TENACITY OF PURPOSE

Squadron 100 pilot Haim Ezekiel departed Ktziot at 0600 and was already approaching the end of his mission when he faced a dilemma, as presented in his debrief:

> At 1230, after I had already finished patrol and was on my way back, over Jabel Libni, I was informed that... a force of ours, with 20 tanks, was about to attack an Egyptian force with 100 tanks; I was tasked to stop them from attacking but my fuel state suggested that this was impossible to accomplish. I decided to deliver the message; my consideration was that if I would run out fuel then I would land beside our forces and would wait for fuel. I landed beside the column [of ILDF tanks] in time to stop them, just before they were about to start moving. Fuel sufficed for RTB.

RUNWAY UNIT AT BIR HAMA

1300–1615	100	Piper	Zusman	Beer Sheba–Bir Hama–Quseima–Beer Sheba

In debrief, Isaac Zusman reported:

> Landed at Bir Hama where a runway unit had just arrived; picked up a message for delivery to Quseima; waited at Quseima half an hour because local commander was not

A Squadron 100 Piper over ILDF troops, reportedly over Sinai during the Suez War. Squadron 100 Pipers served ILDF divisions and battalions as eyes, ears and hacks, in most missions flying with ILDF scouts specifically trained for patrol from the air.

ILDF troops at an EGAF airfield in Sinai, possibly Bir Hama or Bir Gafgafa.

Squadron 116 P-51s were tasked to attack the Gaza Strip around sunset during Day 4. This photo of a P-51 being loaded with two bombs and six rockets was taken after 0600 on 2 November 1956 as the P-51 is marked with ILAF Suez War IFF stripes version 2.

there; flew pilot [Eldad] Paz from Quseima to Beer Sheba...

PHOTOGRAPH JORDAN

| 1330–1507 | 115 | Mosquito Kaf8 | photograph Jordan |

MIOR Kaf8 tasked Squadron 115 to photograph Jordan with a Mosquito equipped with a 36in camera. Squadron 115's laboratory accepted the film at 1537 and produced 38 negatives and 114 prints, with data distribution from 1735 and prints posted from 1835.

SUPPORT BULGARIA

1400–	117	Meteor	Altman	support Bde 27
1400–	117	Meteor	Gat	ditto
1500–	113	Ouragan	Halivni	support Div 38
1500–1550	113	4042	Ivry	ditto
1500–	113	Ouragan	Harlev	ditto
1500–	113	Ouragan	Ayalon	ditto

The ILDF noted, at 1430, a Brigade 27 request for air support for armor attack against BULGARIA. IOKR indicated that Squadron 113 pilots were briefed to attack an enemy armor force near Ruefa Dam, south-east of Abu Ageila, but the Ouragan pilots identified ILDF troops at the designated point of attack so they did not attack. Brigade 7 FAC Asher Lavi reported:

> At 1500 I was ordered to contact ILAF aircraft attacking Om Kattef in order to inform them about an enemy column [seemingly] ready for breakthrough [attack] along road, four kilometers from Abu Ageila and where our forces are. I saw the aircraft, I heard them conversing with another FAC but they did not answer my calls [probably because radio malfunctioned]. They circled overhead, twice, but did not open fire at us [Brigade 7 HQ at Abu Ageila]. From their conversation I realized that they were not sure where the enemy was and decided to RTBed...

IOKR indicated that the Ouragan pilots were then retasked to support Brigade 27 at BULGARIA but did not receive orders from FAC and RTBed, while David Ivry reported:

> Support to our forces at Abu Ageila pocket; hits in tail and wing.

At 1510 the ILDF noted interception of the EGDF's Armor Brigade 1 radio messages in Russian, and at 1530 the ILDF Chief of Staff directed that Brigade 11 would replace Brigade 1 at Rafah and take over responsibility for attacking the Gaza Strip, while Brigade 1 would join Brigade 27 in an advance west along RADISH.

BULGARIA OCCUPATION

1535–1615	113	4044	Sheffer	support Bde 7
1535–	113	Ouragan	Furman	ditto
1535–	113	4029	Kishon	ditto
1535–	113	Ouragan	Rosen	ditto

The ILDF noted, at 1555, Brigade 27's report that BULGARIA was in their hands.

OURAGANS OVER BIR GAFGAFA

1620–	113	Ouragan	Hod	support Bde 7
1620–	113	Ouragan	Dan	ditto
1620–	113	Ouragan	Zahavi	ditto
1620–	113	Ouragan	Yariv	ditto

IOKR indicated that Ouragans attacked EGDF armor in the Bir Gafgafa sector; IOKB's only reported attack after 1425 was at 1745, at Bir Gafgafa, with the claimed destruction of five tanks and two tracked vehicles.

GAZA STRIP TARGETING

1630–1720	116	2373	Yavneh	support Bde 11
1630–	116	P-51	Rafaeli	ditto
1630–1720	116	2338	Eyal	ditto
1630–	116	P-51	Kohorn	ditto

Squadron 115 Commander Eli Eyal flew as sub-leader and the formation was tasked to attack targets in the Gaza Strip but no targets, not even alternative targets, were issued prior to take-off and at this phase Brigade 11 had no FAC, while other Division 77 FACs were probably busy elsewhere so the formation was not assigned with targets. The ILAF Central Control Unit suggested that the P-51 pilots would look for fortifications but it was already twilight so

visibility was poor and no fortifications were pinpointed. Then it was suggested that one pair would climb to 3,500 feet in order to attract AAA fire and thus reveal EGDF positions; fiery AAA fire was indeed encountered but no EGDF targets were pinpointed. Central Control Unit ordered them to attack Gaza police station but this target was not identified either, so the P-51s attacked Gaza railway station and RTBed.

FROM SUNSET TO MIDNIGHT

103	1404	Ben Josef/Reubeni/Saul/Bass Tel Nof–Teman Field–JAMAICA–Tel Nof
103	1406	Shabty/Ostashinski/ Tel Nof–Teman Field– (JAMAICA) – Tel Nof, abort Goldreich/Strasman
103	1412	Biran/Vossman Kaf10 Tel Nof–JAMAICA–Tel Nof
103	1414	Biham/Sela/Vronski/Bok Kaf10
103	1418	Ohad/Rom
103	1428	Oz/Biran Kaf10 Tel Nof–JAMAICA–Tel Nof
103	1430)	Avisar/Eyal Kaf10 JAMAICA
103	1430)	Shamir/Michaeli Tel Nof JAMAICA–Tel Nof
103	1432	Kohen/Richter Kaf10 Tel Nof–Teman Field– JAMAICA–Tel Nof
110	2176	Shemer/(Hillel) reconnaissance Jordan Syria
119	3850	Tsiddon/Brosh scramble to intercept

The ILDF plan to replace a Brigade 202 battalion during the night of 31 October to 1 November was not accomplished so an alternative plan was set for the night of 1 to 2 November. Squadron 103 was tasked to airlift a battalion from Teman Field to JAMAICA and return Battalion 890 from JAMAICA to Tel Nof; while engaged in this mission, 1406 experienced engine malfunction, over Sinai,

FRAF Noratlas airlifters augmented ILAF Squadron 103 three Noratlases for drop of supplies to Brigade 202. The FRAF Noratlases were based in Cyprus so staged via Tel Nof, where supplies were loaded and a Squadron 103 navigator joined the French crew in order to improve coordination. This image of a FRAF Noratlas was taken in Israel, possibly at Ramat David, during the Suez War even though the airlifter is not marked with Suez War stripes.

during its flight from Teman Field to JAMAICA, the crew aborted the mission and returned to Tel Nof. In the end, Squadron 103 did not airlift Battalion 890 from JAMAICA to Tel Nof, while some C-47s returned from JAMAICA with casualties.

Fighting practically paused during the nighttime so the ILDF exploited the evening to prepare for Day 5. At 1700, ILDF/G/ Operations translated an ILDF Chief of Staff directive – that Brigade 11 would replace Brigade 1 at Rafah and would take over responsibility for attacking the Gaza Strip, while Brigade 1 would join Brigade 27 in an advance west along RADISH – to an order issued to Command South. At 1800, Squadron 100 ordered the flight at Magen to move from Magen to Beer Sheba in readiness for deployment to El Arish, as it was expected that the Egyptian airfield would be occupied during Day 5. At 1900, the ILDF noted a report from Brigade 202 that EGAF Meteors attacked JAMAICA; it is not known if this report referred to an earlier daytime attack or to an attack past sunset.

Not all fighting paused during nighttime and at 1930 the ILDF noted a request for air support from an unspecified force engaged in fighting at Rafah, but the ILAF's ability to support the ILDF at night – especially when opposing forces were in contact – was very, very limited; it is possible that Squadron 140 was tasked to illuminate but attack aircraft were not scrambled.

Possibly in context of illumination over Rafah, Squadron 103 indicated, at 2030, transfer of flares from illumination readiness aircraft 1411 to 1401; the explanation was noted at 2230 when it was reported that 1411 would not be serviceable until 0300. Also at 2030, Squadron 103 was ordered to prepare, immediately, the psywar loudspeakers C-47 for flight with flares, so it is possible that the psywar loudspeakers C-47 was 1401. Sometime after 2200, Squadron 103 acknowledged the message to delay departure of psywar loudspeakers C-47 until further notice.

At 2300, Tel Nof noted that Squadron 203 finished drop of supplies to forces at JAMAICA.

AIR4 INTELLIGENCE REPORT NUMBER 14

Issued at 2300, AIR4 Intelligence Report Number 14 followed Intelligence Report Number 13 that was issued at 1845 and the two reports presented the picture as known to the ILDF – or evaluated by the ILDF – at the time:

– Brigade 4 was tasked to replace Brigade 202 along CARROT.
– Brigade 7 was along SPINACH east of Bir Gafgafa, facing the EGDF's Armor Brigade 1.
– Brigade 9 was tasked to occupy Sharm El Sheikh.
– Brigade 11 – with a Brigade 37 battalion – was tasked to occupy the Gaza Strip.
– Brigade 27 and Brigade 1 were along RADISH between Rafah and El Arish.
– Brigade 37 and Brigade 10 were still east of CHINA.
– Brigade 202 was along CARROT but planned to advance along BENCH in the direction of Sharm El Sheikh.

ILDF evaluation of the EGDF was that a retreat order was issued to units in Sinai:

– Division 3 was ordered to retreat from the El Arish/Rafah sector along RADISH.
– Division 4 Armor Brigade 1 was in defensive deployment at

Bir Gafgafa after losing some 50 tanks.
– Division 8 was ordered to retreat from the Gaza Strip.
– Battalion 5 that defended Mitle Pass suffered heavy losses.
– Battalion 21 was ordered to retreat from Sharm El Sheikh along BENCH.

ILDF plans for Day 5 were to occupy the Gaza Strip and the Om Kattef pocket, advance to the Suez Canal in parallel efforts along RADISH and SPINACH, and advance to Sharm El Sheikh in a pincer movement with Brigade 9 advancing along the Gulf of Aqaba coast of Sinai and Brigade 202 advancing along the Gulf of Suez coast of Sinai.

Day 5
2 NOVEMBER 1956

ILAF operations during Day 4 practically slowed down and FRAF squadrons in Israel – Squadron 199, Squadron 200 and Squadron 201 – flew most of the offensive missions over west Sinai, practically in support of Anglo-French ground forces tasked to occupy the Suez Canal. While the EGDF was retreating from the ILDF, the Egyptian forces were actually advancing in the direction of Anglo-French forces. Therefore, FRAF attacks over west Sinai during Day 4 were actually interdiction in support of Anglo-French forces and the only ILAF attacks over west Sinai during Day 4 were along BED, which was not a longitudinal axis leading to the Suez Canal but a lateral axis connecting longitudinal axis SPINACH with longitudinal axis CARROT. The ILAF interdicted BED after the ILDF evaluated that elements of the EGDF's Armor Brigade 1 were advancing along BED in order to retreat to the Suez Canal via CARROT and/or to attack Brigade 202 – helpless against an armored force – from east to west. As indicated, the ILAF indeed interdicted BED during Day 4 but by then Egypt prioritized defense of the Suez Canal over defense of Sinai and the EGDF did not attack Brigade 202 along BED and CARROT. The same was expected for Day 5, with the EGDF retreating to the Suez Canal – or, depending upon perspective, advancing in the direction of Anglo-French forces – and the ILAF supporting the ILDF in the Gaza Strip, east Sinai and south Sinai.

FROM MIDNIGHT TO SUNRISE

	103	1409	Shalev/Ofer/Zioni
			drop Flotilla 13 team
	103	1416	Shabty/Ostashinski/
			Tel Nof–JAMAICA–Tel Nof
			Goldreich/Strasman
	103	1432	Kohen/Richter
			Kaf10 Tel Nof–Teman Field–
			JAMAICA–Tel Nof
0200 –	103	C-47	Ganot
			Kaf11 psywar Gaza Strip

The airlift to JAMAICA continued; the battalion flown from Teman Field to JAMAICA was most likely Brigade 4's Battalion 42, while at 0025 the ILDF noted an order to return the battalion that was originally planned for airlift to JAMAICA, from Tel Nof to mother unit Brigade 11.

The ILAF planned to activate emergency airfields at already-

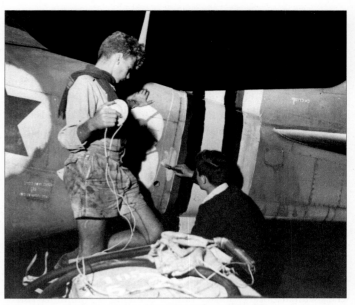

Squadron 116 servicemen painting ILAF Suez War IFF stripes version 2 on P-51 38, most likely during the night of 1 to 2 November 1956. ILAF Suez War IFF stripes version 2 were in force from 0600 on 2 November 1956.

occupied Bir Hama and yet-to-be-occupied El Tor and El Arish. In this context, AIR1 ordered, at 0130, activation, at Tel Nof, of Runway Branch Unit 322 and Runway Branch Unit 810; the latter was planned to deploy to El Tor.

IOKR indicated that psywar C-47 departed Tel Nof at 0200 and broadcast calls to surrender over the Gaza Strip, but Squadron 103 noted, at circa 0230, that MIOR Kaf11 was canceled. Later on, Squadron 103 reported that psywar C-47 loudspeakers had to be fixed.

RECONNAISSANCE JORDAN/SYRIA

| 0255–0525 | 110 | 2169 | Levin/Hy |
| | | | Kaf2 reconnaissance Jordan/Syria |

Israel monitored military activity in Jordan and Syria throughout Operation KADESH. Squadron 110 Mosquitoes mostly flew visual reconnaissance missions over Jordan and Syria during nighttime; MIOR Kaf2 debrief reported:

> Flew from base to Bnot Jacob Bridge and from there over road to Damascus. At 0320, some 20 kilometers south-west of Damascus, a two-section convoy was sighted. Each section composed 24 vehicles with lights on; distance between sections was two kilometers. The convoy headed to Quneitra. At 0340 a convoy that composed more than 20 vehicles was sighted along road from Amman to Salt. From Salt, flew north to Allenby Bridge, then north, along River Jordan, to Sea of Galilee and from there to Daraa. At 0453, sighted, some 40 kilometers south-west of Damascus, some 20 vehicles in a convoy that headed to Quneitra; this was probably part of the above-mentioned convoy.

BOMBING GAZA

0410–	69	1623	Ben Haim	
			Kaf13 support Div 77	
0410–0555	69	1622	Efrat/Josefon	ditto

Squadron 69 accepted AIR3 MIOR Kaf13 at 0225. MIOR Kaf13 tasked Squadron 69 to bomb El Arish but, in a phone call, the AIR3 Chief changed the target to bomb RADISH in order to disrupt the EGDF retreat. This change of mission posed a problem for Squadron 69, as optimum armament for the new mission would have been semi armor-penetration bombs with 0.3 to 0.7 seconds delay detonators, but these were not available at Ramat David so bombers were loaded with 250 kilograms general purpose bombs with 0.1 seconds delay fuses.

Eventually, the B-17s bombed Gaza. To assist the bombers, an Israeli village was illuminated as Initial Point for final run and the plan was that the trailing bomber would bomb five minutes after the lead bomber. Low clouds, at an altitude of 3,500 feet, covered the sky along the route from Ramat David to Gaza and prevented visual contact between bombers. This was obviously not critical if the plan had been adhered to, but Central Control Unit rushed the two crews to bomb Gaza ASAP. The pilots changed headings and speeded up, but this disrupted bombing. The two bombers were heading towards Gaza with identical estimated time of bombing. To minimize risk of collision, the leader split the target into two sectors, with the trailing bomber targeting the northern outskirts of Gaza and the leading bomber focusing on the southern part of the city. As a result, the center of Gaza was not bombed as planned and bombs were scattered over the outskirts of the city.

The ILDF noted, at 0500, that Brigade 11 had already initiated an attack against the Gaza Strip and, perhaps for this reason, Central Control Unit rushed Squadron 69 crews.

OCCUPATION EL ARISH

0500–	105	P-51	Kopel	support Bde 11
0500–0710	105	2339	Niv	ditto
0500–	105	P-51	Pressman	ditto
0500–	105	P-51	Helman	ditto
0501–0711	105	2369	Bodilewski	support Bde 11
0501–	105	P-51	Hagani	ditto
0501–	105	P-51	Shaked	ditto
0501–	105	P-51	Melamed	ditto

IOKR indicated that the first formation established contact with FAC and attacked, but the second formation was unable to establish contact with FAC so did not attack. Perhaps the second formation was retasked to interdict along RADISH, as Isaiah Bodilewski reported:

> Attack convoys along El Arish road, [claimed destruction of one] tank [and one] tracked vehicle.

IOKB reported that eight P-51s attacking El Arish at 0545 hit two ammunition stores.

IOKR indicated that a Brigade 11 force occupied Gaza at 0600 and a Brigade 27 force attacked El Arish from 0500 until 0630; the ILDF noted, at 0600, a message from Division 77 that ILDF troops entered El Arish, and messages that El Arish had been occupied were noted from 0630 until 0650.

EGDF ARMOR BRIGADE 1 RETREAT

0550–	200	F-84F	interdiction RADISH

Brigade 27 occupied El Arish air base at about 0630 on 2 November 1956. El Arish air base salvage yard reminded many of the 1948 Arab-Israeli War, with a few dumped Italian-made fighters that operated from El Arish back in 1948.

0600–0707	101 silver1	4529	Egozi	reconnaissance SPINACH
0600–0707	101 silver2	4533	Shavit	ditto

Squadron 200 dispatched three formations, with 14 sorties, until 0910, to interdict EGDF troops along RADISH who were retreating from the ILDF in Sinai and advancing in the direction of Anglo-French forces in the north sector of the Suez Canal. IOKB reported that F-84Fs attacking along RADISH, south of Bardavil, at 0600, claimed the destruction of 12 vehicles, while F-84Fs attacking along RADISH, about four kilometers east of Romani, at 0635, claimed to have destroyed one tank, one towed gun and three trucks.

Squadron 101's silver section recced SPINACH and reported that the EGDF's Armor Brigade 1 was in retreat.

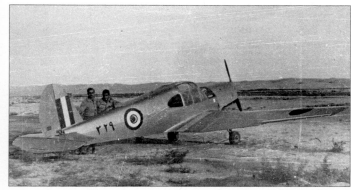

Squadron 113 pilot David Ivry flew Ouragan 45 to interdict RADISH on the morning of 2 November 1956; 4045 was photographed in typical Ouragan Suez War configuration, with two napalm canisters and eight rockets.

In addition to aircraft wreckages at the salvage yard and Vampire dummies in pens at El Arish, the ILDF captured a few seemingly intact Czechoslovakian Sokol lightplanes, including EGAF Number 329.

BRIGADE 7 ATTACK BIR GAFGAFA

0620–	110	2184	Ash/ Segal	support Bde 11
0620–0850	110	2168	Proshanski	ditto
0620–	110	Mosquito		ditto
0620–	110	Mosquito Eyal		ditto
0715–	110	Mosquito Fuchs		support Bde 11
0715–	110	Mosquito Bavli		ditto

The ILDF noted, at 0630, a message from FAC Mobile Number 13 that El Arish airfield had been occupied – by Brigade 27 – and another message from FAC network that Brigade 7 was attacking Bir Gafgafa.

The Gaza Strip was already being invaded by Brigade 11 so Squadron 110 Mosquitoes were diverted to interdict along RADISH, bombing a road bridge nearby Romani, possibly in order to stop the EGDF retreat/advance in direction of Qantara and Anglo-French forces; according to IOKB they attacked at 0750. Also retasked to interdict RADISH, IOKB reported that the two Mosquitoes attacked at 0843 and hit a train.

OURAGANS INTERDICT RADISH

0755–	113	Ouragan Sharon	interdiction RADISH	
0755–	113	Ouragan Rosen	ditto	
0755–	113	Ouragan Lidor	ditto	
0755–	113	Ouragan Ayalon	ditto	
0800–	113	Ouragan Halivni	interdiction RADISH	
0800–	113	4045	Ivry	ditto

The first formation observed some six tanks nearby Qantara and

Squadron 116 pilot Dan Barak flew P-51 03 on a mission to support Brigade 37 on the morning of 2 November 1956.

claimed the destruction of eight vehicles. The second formation claimed to have destroyed two armored vehicles, one fuel tanker and a truck.

OCCUPATION OM SHIKHAN

0840–1120	116	2303	Barak	support Bde 37
0840–	116	P-51	Bloch	ditto
0840–	116	2312	Sharon	ditto
0840–	116	P-51	Kohorn	ditto

Brigade 37 was again tasked to occupy CHINA, with Squadron 116 to attack Om Shikhan fort ahead of Brigade 37's attack. P-51s attacked but the fort seemed deserted, which the formation leader reported to Division 38 ALO Israel Ben-Shahar. The ILDF noted, at 1000, a report from Brigade 10 that the Om Kattef fortifications were not returning fire and that forces started to move in the direction of the fortifications. Brigade 37 attacked – every now and then the forces stopped and called for air support – and occupied Om Shikhan, which was indeed empty as the EGDF had retreated from fort. The ILDF noted, at 1130, a message from Division 38 that the Om Kattef locality had been occupied.

RAID TABLE

0855–	113	Ouragan	Hod	support
0855–	113	Ouragan	Furman	ditto
0855–	113	Ouragan	Harlev	ditto
0855–	113	Ouragan	Dan	ditto

IOKR reported that Ouragans raided enemy forces along TABLE between El Arish and Jabel Libni.

ATTACK KHAN YUNES

0900–	117	Meteor	Yoeli	support Bde 11
0900–	117	Meteor	Alroy	ditto
0900–0945	117	3605	Kaspit	support Bde 11
0900–0945	117	3606	Yahalom	ditto

The first pair was tasked to attack Khan Yunes. The second pair was tasked to attack Gaza, but also attacked Khan Yunes.

STATUS REPORT

105	2354	Bodilewski	test
115	1168	Tavor	test
115	2190	Tavor	test

ILDF/G/Operations reported the situation as it was at 0900:

– Brigade 4 replaced two Brigade 202 companies.
– Brigade 7 occupied Bir Gafgafa junction along SPINACH.
– Brigade 9 advancing in the direction of Sharm El Sheikh.
– Brigade 11 attacked the Gaza Strip from 0500; Gaza surrendered at 0900; next objective was to occupy Khan Yunes.
– Brigade 27 occupied El Arish at 0745 and was advancing west along RADISH.

INTERDICTION SPINACH

0915–1020	101	4584	Peled	interdiction green1 SPINACH
0915–1020	101green2	4590	Ronen	ditto
0915–1020	101green3	4562	Morgan	ditto
0915–1020	101greed4	4561	Golan	ditto
0915–1015	113	4050	Sheffer	interdiction SPINACH
0915–	113	Ouragan	Zahavi	ditto
0915–	113	4074	Kishon	ditto
0915–	113	Ouragan	Yariv	ditto
0920–1010	101blue1	4560	Nevo	interdiction SPINACH
0930–1035	101blue2	4549	Zuk	ditto
0930–1035	101blue3	4543	Lev	ditto
0930–1035	101blue4	4563	Lapidot	ditto
0935–1035	101blue1	4552	Gonen	ditto

Squadron 101 Mystère pilots and Squadron 113 Ouragan pilots attacked the EGDF's Armor Brigade 1 during its retreat along SPINACH between Bir Gafgafa and Ismailia. Squadron 113 pilots claimed the destruction of two tanks and five vehicles.

INTERDICTION RADISH

0925–	113	Ouragan	Bareket	interdiction RADISH
0925–	113	Ouragan	Weizman	ditto
0925–1025	113	4044	Agassi	ditto
0925–	113	Ouragan	Erez	ditto

BIR HAMA AIRFIELD ACTIVATION

	103	C-47	Yaffe	Tel Nof–Bir Hama– Tel Nof
103	1402		Biran/Vossman	Tel Nof–Bir Hama– Tel Nof

Squadron 103 noted, at 0810, a directive to dispatch a C-47 to Megiddo, where Runway Unit 757 was deployed; the C-47 was to fly Runway Branch Unit 509 from Megiddo to Tel Nof and thence to Bir Hama, in line with MIOR Kaf9, so that Runway Branch Unit 509 would operate Bir Hama airfield. Tel Nof noted, at 0930, that a Noratlas was just about to depart Tel Nof on a flight to Bir Hama while a C-47 would fly from Tel Nof to Megiddo to airlift equipment from Megiddo to Bir Hama.

PHOTOGRAPH EL ARISH

0940–1055	115	3517	Livneh/ Galon Kaf16 photograph El Arish

The ILAF accepted ILDF/I requirement at 0530; AIR3 issued MIOR Kaf16 at 0725; Squadron 115 flew the mission in a Meteor trainer equipped with a 36in camera. At the time of the requirement's issue, El Arish was not yet in ILDF hands, but it was by the time

Squadron 101 pilot Zorik Lev flew Mystère 43 to interdict SPINACH on the morning of 2 November 1956.

Squadron 113 Deputy A Jacob Agassi departed Hatzor, at 0925, on 2 November 1956, in Ouragan 44 to interdict RADISH.

Squadron 115 pilot Zeev Tavor and navigator Arie Raviv flew visual reconnaissance over the Red Sea and Sinai coastline, in a photographic reconnaissance Mosquito, on 2 November 1956.

the mission was flown. Negatives were handed over to Squadron 115's laboratory at 1050, the lab processed 68 frames and produced 204 prints, data distribution was initiated at 1310 and prints posting started at 1335.

ATTACK OR NOT?

0945–	105	P-51	Kopel	support Bde 11
0945–1215	105	P-51	Zur	ditto
0945–	105	P-51	Shaked	ditto
0945–1210	105	2326	Dagan	ditto

IOKR indicated that P-51s were tasked to attack Khan Yunes but were diverted – or retasked – to the Abu Ageila sector where no EGDF targets were pinpointed, so the four P-51s RTBed without attacking at all. Both wingmen – Arie Dagan and Levy Zur – reported that the formation attacked but did not specify what or where.

SUPPRESS SHARM EL SHEIKH

	115	2132	Tavor/Raviv	
		reconnaissance Sharm El Sheikh–El Tor		
1030 –	105	P-51		
		attack Ras Nasrani		
1030 –1340	105	2310	Ben-Nun	ditto
1030 –	105	P-51	Pressman	ditto
1030 –	105	P-51	Maor	ditto
1050 –	69	1623)	Ben–Haim/(Narunski)	
		attack Sharm El Sheikh		
1050 –1720	69	1622	Efrat/Josefon	ditto
1100 –1425	110	2168	Orli/Levy	
		attack Sharm El Sheikh		
1100 –	110	2175	Shemer	ditto
1100 –1425	110	2169	Levin/Dishoni	ditto
1100 –	110	Mosquito	Landau	ditto

Brigade 9 advanced along challenging terrain and poor paths from Ras Naqab, north-west of Eilat, to Sharm El Sheikh at the southern tip of Sinai, a net distance of more than 200 kilometers. By Day 5, the main body of Brigade 9 was some 150 kilometers from Sharm El Sheikh and the ILDF evaluated options to expedite the occupation of Sharm El Sheikh; Operation KADESH 6 order was issued during

Squadron 69 pilot Reuben Narunski (right) inspects the Aircraft Servicing Form 4420 of 1623 prior to departure from Ramat David on a mission to bomb Sharm El Sheikh, on 2 November 1956. The Squadron 110 Mosquito in the background is possibly 2184.

Squadron 110 pilot Dave Orli and navigator Haim Levy flew Mosquito 68 to attack Sharm El Sheikh on 2 November 1956. Photographed at Ramat David with typical Suez War Mosquito configuration - bombs and rockets - the depicted Mosquito is possibly 2168 or 2178.

Day 5 and ordered Brigade 202 to advance from Mitle to El Tor and thence to Sharm El Sheikh along BENCH. The first phase covered the drop of a company over El Tor – some 100 kilometers from Sharm El Sheikh – and subsequent airlift to El Tor of two battalions. At about the same time, Squadron 103 would drop a company over Sharm El Sheikh. As indicated in AIR4 Intelligence Report Number 16, ILDF/I evaluation was that the Sharm El Sheikh garrison was ordered to retreat to the Suez Canal along BENCH, so that by the time of the drop, Sharm El Sheikh would be empty; the dropped company would hold Sharm El Sheikh until the arrival of either Brigade 9, along the east coast of Sinai, or Brigade 202, along the west coast of Sinai. The ILDF noted, at 1030, that the assault of El Tor had been planned and initial orders had been issued. In this context, the ILAF was probably ordered to suppress Sharm El Sheikh as well as its outpost Ras Nasrani, north-east of Sharm El Sheikh along the advance route of Brigade 9. Since ILAF action was planned as preparation fire for Squadron 103's drop, and since Brigade 9 was still quite far from Ras Nasrani, Brigade 9 ALO and FACs were not informed that the ILAF was attacking Ras Nasrani and Sharm El Sheikh.

Additionally, the ILAF tasked a Squadron 115 Mosquito to visually recce sectors of Sharm El Sheikh and El Tor. IOKR stated:

> Squadron 115 performed on Friday, 2 November 1956, one photographic reconnaissance over Straits of Tiran sector… Photographs revealed Egyptian posts at Ras Nasrani, infrastructures and artillery at Sharm El Sheikh, and movement of two vehicles.

However, only one photographic reconnaissance mission was reported during Day 5 and no photographic laboratory processed, printed and posted photos from the Sharm El Sheikh sector on 2 November. The mission was almost certainly visual reconnaissance and not photographic reconnaissance; navigator Arie Raviv remembered a low altitude flight along the coastline up to Abu Rhodes, as well as fiery AAA fire. Brigade 9 ALO Elijah Rosen reported:

> I demanded a visual reconnaissance along route from El Tor to Sharm El Sheikh in order to inspect arrival of reinforcements as well as to scan sea for presence of warships. This was accomplished and [visual recce] results were reported to us over FAC [radio] network. At the same time – as we learnt later – our aircraft attacked Ras Nasrani and Sharm El Sheikh and tried to contact us. Since I was not informed [that the ILAF was about to attack Ras Nasrani and Sharm El Sheikh], I was not listening [on the radio] so there was no [radio] contact [between Brigade 9 ALO/FAC and ILAF aircraft operating over Ras Nasrani and Sharm El Sheikh]…

The first formations tasked to suppress the Sharm El Sheikh sector probably departed Ramat David. IOKR did not mention the four Squadron 105 P-51s that bombed, rocketed and strafed Ras Nasrani – most likely an unintentional omission – but IOKB indicated that the four P-51s attacking Ras Nasrani at 1150 claimed the destruction of one AAA gun and several buildings.

Likewise, IOKR indicated that two B-17s tasked to bomb Sharm El Sheikh departed Ramat David at 1230, but IOKB reported that B-17s bombed Sharm El Sheikh at 1300; obviously such a short timeframe between take-off and attack was impossible to accomplish since it took

the B-17s more than two hours to fly from Ramat David to Sharm El Sheikh, so either the pair took off around 1100 or attacked circa 1430. Either way, Squadron 69's post-war report indicated that AIR3 did not initially define which target to attack at Sharm El Sheikh, so Squadron 69 analyzed available intelligence data and came to the conclusion that there were three valid targets: the airfield, barracks and port. Squadron 69 consulted with the Ramat David Wing 1 Commander, which led to a decision to bomb the barracks and port.

Eventually, AIR3 notified Squadron 69 that the target was the barracks, but by then the B-17s were already loaded with a mix of 250 kilograms and 50 kilograms bombs suitable for bombing the barracks and port; there was no time to change to only 250 kilograms bombs.

In order to confuse AAA, bombers arrived simultaneously from different directions. The Israelis expected that this tactic would split AAA attention between the two bombers, but Egyptian AAA figured otherwise and concentrated fire at the lead B-17. The bombers were equipped with Mark 9 sights that required the crew to fly a steady bomb run at a constant altitude and speed for at least 20 to 30 seconds. It was during this bomb run that 1623 was hit. Gunner Gideon Shenhav recalled:

> AAA fire hit us over Sharm El Sheikh and we had a very tedious flight coming back home. At first it looked like smoke but when I had a closer look from the ball turret I realized it was fuel leaking from the main tank. The pilot immediately feathered a prop and shut off this tank. One main fuel tank was severely damaged and we came back almost with no fuel left for a go around [if this had to be flown]; upon landing, at the end of the runway, the last engine cut out. Checking out the wing, we observed a huge hole where the munitions went through.

Again, IOKR indicated that the four Mosquitoes tasked to bomb Sharm El Sheikh departed Ramat David at 1215 but IOKB reported that the Mosquitoes attacked at 1230 and claimed the destruction of one half-track; obviously such a short time between take-off and attack was impossible to accomplish since it took the Mosquitoes some 90 minutes to fly from Ramat David to Sharm ElS heikh, so either the Mosquitoes took off around 1100 or attacked circa 1345. IOKR stated that one Mosquito malfunctioned en route to the target, aborted its mission and landed at Tel Nof, while three Mosquitoes attacked and landed to refuel at Hatzor on the way back to Ramat David; this was probably partially correct, since Dave Orli reported a direct flight back to Ramat David but Amity Levin reported a flight to Hatzor and thence to Ramat David. Hatzor Wing 4 Commander Ezer Weizman exploited the landing of the Mosquito at Hatzor for a direct debrief concerning the situation at Sharm El Sheikh.

AIR4 INTELLIGENCE REPORT NUMBER 16

	100	0471		Lod– (Ramla)
11:30-	100	0450	Finkelstein	(Eilat)El Tor–Ramla

Issued at 1115, AIR4 Intelligence Report Number 16 indicated that EGDF units in the Gaza Strip had surrendered, that El Arish had been occupied and all EGDF units in Sinai – except forces encircled at the Om Shikhan fortifications south-east of Abu Ageila – were in retreat to the Suez Canal, while the garrison at Sharm El Sheikh was already preparing to retreat along BENCH. This ILDF/I evaluation was not wholly correct, as not all EGDF units in the Gaza Strip had

Squadron 100 Flight A, at Ramla, accepted Piper 53 on 30 October 1956; 0453 subsequently served with Squadron 100's main body at Beer Sheba.

A Squadron 100 Piper on a road in Sinai beside ILDF half-tracks. The ILDF tasked Squadron 100's main body at Beer Sheba as well as flights attached to Division 38 and Division 77 and Pipers deployed to Eilat. Pipers' main missions during the Suez War were communication, patrol, transport and CASEVAC.

surrendered and fighting in the Khan Yunes sector was still raging, the EGDF unit supposedly encircled east of Abu Ageila had already managed to retreat and the retreat of the Sharm El Sheikh garrison along BENCH was an unlikely option due to ILAF air superiority and ILDF plans to advance along BENCH from Mitle to El Tor and thence to Sharm El Sheikh.

BRIGADE 7 VERSUS BRIGADE 37

100	Piper	Sirotkin/Scout	support Div 38
117	Meteor	BenAaron	support Div 38
117	Meteor	Alroy	ditto

The ILDF was unaware that supposedly-encircled EGDF troops in the CHINA locality – with Brigade 7 west of CHINA and Brigades 10 and 37 east of CHINA – had retreated during the night of 1 to 2 November, so that Brigades 10 and 37's attack from east to west was against deserted and empty fortifications. Brigade 37 armor therefore advanced, from east to west, much faster than could have been anticipated, while the advance of Brigade 37 seemed to Brigade 7's Battalion 82 as an EGDF effort to break through the supposed blockade.

The ILDF noted, at 1200, a message from Division 38 that Brigade 7's Battalion 82 tanks engaged in battle Brigade 10 – actually Brigade 37 – tanks. If timing of this message was correct, then this 'friendly fire' incident occurred some time before 1200. Earlier, at 1000, the Squadron 100 diary noted that two ILDF armor forces were engaged in a 'friendly fire' incident. Squadron 100 pilot Paltiel Sirotkin reported:

An order to paint new IFF stripes was received on 2 November [– Squadron 100 diary indicated receipt of MAT3 repaint order at 0910 and it is likely that the flight at Nitzana was notified some time later] and flying [aircraft with old IFF stripes] was banned except for flight [from Nitzana] to Beer Sheba if impossible to paint [at Nitzana]. An order to take-off immediately was received at about the same time.

Our forces attacked Om Shikhan from two sides, one force from Nitzana and one from Abu Ageila. Enemy forces escaped during nighttime so [the] armor that attacked from Nitzana and overran Om Shikhan encountered our forces at the side of Abu Ageila. It was then that we received an order to take-off immediately in order to cease fire between our forces.

From 2 November 1956 onwards, Squadron 100 Pipers also landed at El Arish and Bir Hama, to where Division 77 Flight and Division 38 Flight deployed, respectively.

Mission was so crucial that I took off in an aircraft that had not been repainted with new IFF stripes. I immediately flew in between forces and ceased fire because both forces saw a [friendly] Piper in front of them. I then landed near attacking force, in the side of Abu Ageila, in an inconvenient place to land, a road in a gorge, very close to our attacking force and with a burnt-out tank in the middle of the road at the start of the landing run. I managed to land exactly near [the] attacking force, stopped aircraft and informed commander of attacking force to cease fire. I then took off, guided the two forces as they approached one another and flew in between them until they linked up.

I again landed on the road, Division 38 Intelligence Officer replaced scout and we flew along road from Abu Ageila to El Arish because we were informed that our [Division 77] forces occupied El Arish and we wanted to prevent possibility of another ['friendly fire'] incident [between Division 38 and Division 77]. We observed Egyptian forces retreating along road from Abu Ageila to El Arish and landed at El Arish – on a road, not at airfield – to deliver these two messages [that Egyptian forces were retreating from Division 38 sector in direction of Division 77 forces at El Arish and that Division 38 planned to task a force to advance along the road from Abu Ageila to El Arish] and were informed that our forces who had occupied Gaza and Rafah were advancing along [the] Rafah to Nitzana road. We informed both forces about the situation along the road, warned them not to open fire at each other... informed the force at Nitzana and landed.

IOKR indicated that two Meteors departed Tel Nof at 1220, noticed a 'friendly fire' incident, fired several warning bursts and RTBed. If the ILDF note from 1200 was accurate, then the Meteors probably departed Tel Nof earlier; supporting this is another report that Squadron 100 pilot Paltiel Sirotkin departed Nitzana again at 1230. Another perspective to the Meteors' action was given by Brigade 10 FAC Dan Hadani, who reported:

Our tanks attacked our tanks and our aircraft started to attack one column. I immediately ordered aircraft to cease fire and they aborted attack with nearly no damage to our forces.

GREEN 1 DOWN AND BLUE 3 DOWN

1145–	116blue1	P-51	Zeelon	attack Ras Nasrani
1145–1445	116blue2	2343	Fredilis	ditto
1145–1305	116blue3	2373	Etkes	ditto
1145–	116blue4	2329	Cohen	ditto
1200–1230	101 green1	4584	Peled	attack Ras Nasrani
1200–	101 green2	4560	Ronen	ditto
1200–1315	101green3	4529	Avneri	ditto
1200–1315	101green4	4528	Gilboa	ditto
1201–1315	101red1	4552	Shapira	attack Sharm El Sheikh
1201–1315	101red2	4562	Margalit	ditto
1201–1315	101red3	4580	Bar	ditto
1201–1315	101red4	4542	Bet–On	ditto

Squadron 116's blue section departed Tel Nof before Squadron 101's green section departed Hatzor, but the faster Mysteres were the first to attack Ras Nasrani. Beni Peled reported:

AAA fire hit aircraft while attacking Ras Nasrani fortifications. Fire entered cockpit from pressurization ducts behind the seat and adjacent to windshield. I switched off pressurization, fire continued and I decided to abandon aircraft.

I ejected canopy and canopy ejected without a flaw. Immediately afterwards, fire intensified and I immediately lifted handle to ejection loop and pulled forcefully. I did not lower visor but visor probably lowered when I pulled curtain. Seat activated immediately after end of pull and ejected me upwards. All this action was at about 3,000 to 4,000 feet [altitude] after I pulled up from deck after strafing. Immediately after ejection I sensed that seat rolled several times. I released curtain during ejection and it was probably then that [my] helmet and mask were torn away. I separated myself from seat and felt that I was falling forward from seat. I opened parachute manually, probably when my body was horizontal with my face facing down; parachute opened smoothly and I was not rocked. Only then I realized that I [had] lost helmet and mask... I was unable to estimate vertical velocity during drop and it looked like it was slow. I also noticed holes in canopy of parachute. I prepared

Suez War P-51 common configuration was six rockets and two napalm canisters or two bombs. Napalm was mostly preferred for interdiction while bombs - as illustrated - sometimes substituted for napalm when P-51s were tasked to fly attack missions.

Squadron 101 Commander Benjamin Peled in the cockpit of Mystère 84 prior to a mission on 2 November 1956. Peled ejected from 4584 around 1230, the first ILAF pilot ever to eject.

for landing but final phase [of drop] proved to me that vertical velocity was much faster than I figured. My feet hit the ground hard and I performed several rolls. Wind speed was... 20–30 knots. At the end of rolls I released myself from parachute while being dragged along gravel ground and I overturned on my belly in order to release dinghy. I was unable to release second connection and I felt that I was being dragged faster and faster over gravel. I released myself from parachute that was blown away. I retraced, collected my pistol that dropped from pistol sheath during drag, picked up sleeve of parachute and started walking in direction of mountains.

Squadron 101's green 1 was down. Squadron 116 blue section then attacked. Jonathan Etkes recalled:

We approached target when I heard Dror Avneri shouting 'Beni, you are on fire! Beni, eject!'... then I heard Avneri again 'we are running out of fuel; we must return; Beni is close to Egyptian locality; can anyone watch over him?'.

I volunteered and we stayed there, me and my wingman Cheetah [Cohen] as the other two P-51s flew north. I saw the black hole that marked the crash site of Beni's Mystère outside the fence of the fortification at Ras Nasrani and it was obvious that Egyptian troops could have reached him within minutes. We flew low over the water and headed in direction so that sun would blind Egyptians in order to make it more difficult for them to aim at us. We accelerated and fired short bursts so that ammunition would last longer and Beni would have more time to distance from fortification... Sky was full of small black puffs, caused by exploding AAA rounds... It was my fourth mission and I have seen AAA fire before but the fire that shot down Beni, and that was by then aimed at me, was terrible.

While aiming, I noted a streak of fire in my direction... Then I sensed strong shock; an AAA round hit me... I was wounded in my leg. At first I did not feel any pain even though blood was streaming from my leg like water from a tap, my wounded leg jumped from its normal position and was on the stick and the instruments panel was covered with blood. Thinking 'what is my leg doing over here?', I moved my leg from the stick and returned it to normal position.

I was very low, at about 100 feet AGL, so I pulled up but G force impacted me and I sensed that I was losing a lot of blood. It was then that I thought about Uri Schlesinger... Schlesinger was hit on 31 October 1956 but it was not clear if he was wounded or if his aircraft was damaged... Schlesinger continued flying for some time until his aircraft crashed and he was killed; again it was unclear if crash resulted from injury of pilot or from damage to aircraft. I decided not to wait, I decided to land immediately.

I transmitted 'blue 3 emergency landing', released canopy, closed throttle and lowered flaps but I did not have time to perform vital actions, to close fuel valve, to switch off electricity and to switch off engine.

I headed north-east, flying at 110 mph, sea on my right, mountains on my left, when I hit [the ground] hard. The aircraft jumped back into the air but in the second attempt I managed to land... the aircraft stopped north of the fortification, nearby the coast... I opened seat belts, released parachute harness, held chair and wall of the cockpit and pulled myself out. I wanted to run in direction of mountains, as far away as possible from fortification, but I collapsed after a few meters... I saw Cheetah pass over and I waved with my left hand; Cheetah rocked wings and headed north.

Blood was still streaming from my leg. I bandaged the wound with my field dressing and improvised a ligature to stop bleeding but I was still losing blood. I was lying near the aircraft, [which] did not catch fire during landing, and nearby a rocket that did not explode after it detached from the aircraft. I drunk all water from my emergency kit and I was still very thirsty. I felt as though I was fading away when I sensed a shadow. I opened my eyes and saw vultures overhead...

Then something happened; something that never happened to me before or since then. I was fading away when I heard a P-51. I opened my eyes and saw a lone P-51 flying north. I felt as though I was floating upwards, hovering over the P-51 and looking down into the cockpit. In the cockpit, through the canopy, I saw my squadron commander Zahik Yavneh struggling with the stick in order to level the aircraft and eventually binding the oxygen pipe around the stick. I then passed out...

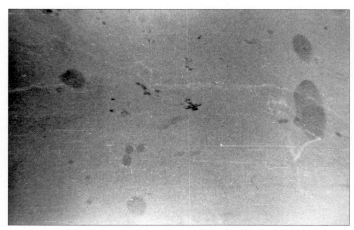

Reportedly a photo of Jonathan Etkes' P-51 73 after landing near Ras Nasrani at about 1305 on 2 November 1956.

Menahem Bar (right) took over as Squadron 101 Commander (Acting) in the wake of Benjamin Peled's ejection from Mystère 84 on 2 November 1956. Hatzor Wing 4 Commander Ezer Weizman is on the left.

I was lying unconscious for several hours until Egyptian troops arrived at about 1700. I was amidst a huge blood puddle so they were probably sure that I was dead. They rolled me with their bayonets and I opened my eyes. The troops were surprised that the supposed dead was very much alive and they backed off, but not for long. They returned and I was sure that they would stab me with their bayonets and shoot me with their rifles; I was sure that this was the end for me. Suddenly, I heard their commander yelling and, standing over me, he practically repelled them and even hit them with the butt of his rifle so that they would not kill me. Finally, he calmed down his soldiers and only then he allowed them to get closer. At first they took my watch, then they took my identification tag and only then they took my pistol...

The officer who saved my life questioned me in English and ordered his soldiers to collect maps from the cockpit. I asked for water but the officer retorted 'We shot down six of your aircraft' and explained that they were tasked to bring the other pilots so they would pick me up on their way back.

I was alone again, in pain, terrible pains, still thirsty, very thirsty, when I saw a Piper descending over the horizon. At first I was relieved to think that Beni was rescued but then I was not sure if the vision was real or an illusion.

A few hours later they [the Egyptians] returned and started to argue; at first I did not know about what were they arguing, I did not understand Arabic. The officer then asked me, in English, 'how are we going to carry you?'. I suggested that they would use my parachute that was still in its pack inside the cockpit; 'that is a good idea' he said and ordered his soldiers to bring the parachute, but the soldiers refused to return to the cockpit, maybe they feared that it was somehow [booby-]trapped. The officer brought the parachute and ordered me to open it... I opened the parachute and they improvised a sort of a hammock. At first they carried me and then they dragged me along on the ground. Suddenly they stopped and looked up; the sky was bright and millions of stars glittered as a lone C-47, with navigation lights on, passed overhead. I did not hear it but I was told that the C-47 was equipped with loudspeakers and broadcast a warning to treat prisoners of war according to the Geneva Convention.

It was evening when we arrived at the camp that I attacked several hours before. They placed me on the floor of a concrete bunker and I, again, asked for water. This time the answer was 'you bombed the water tank, we have no water!'.

RESCUE BENI

1225–1505	116	2353	Yavneh	
		attack Ras Nasrani		
1225–	116	P-51	Hativa	ditto
1225–1525	116	2370	Eyal	ditto
1225–	116	P-51	Rafaeli	ditto
1230–	100	0434	Sirotkin/scout	Nitzana
1250–	110	Mosquito	Somech	
		attack Sharm El Sheikh		
1250–1635	110	2171	Proshanski	ditto
1250–	110	2184	Ash/Segal	ditto
1250–	110	Mosquito	Eyal	ditto
	100	Piper	Greenbaum	
		Eilat–Ras Nasrani–Eilat		
	100	Piper	Hasson Eilat–Eilat	

Around 1300, small arms fire hit Piper 34 over Om Shikhan; 0434 RTBed where four hits were pinpointed.

The ILDF focused on efforts to expedite the occupation of Sharm El Sheikh and to complete capture of Sinai. At 1245, ILDF/G/Operations reported to Brigade 202 that the plan was to drop a Brigade 88 force at El Tor and then to airlift Brigade 112 to El Tor. At 1300, the ILDF

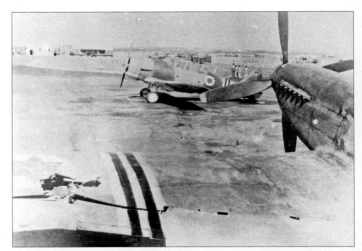

Egyptian AAA fire damaged P-51 53. Squadron 116 Commander Zahik Yavneh flew 2353 all the way from Ras Nasrani to Tel Nof with a holed left wing.

ordered Brigade 202 to advance to Ras Sudar in order to occupy the oil fields. At 1430, the ILDF noted a message from Command South that a Brigade 7 patrol advanced to within 18 kilometers of Ismailia. At 1500, a Brigade 27 force arrived at Romani, some 30 kilometers east of the Suez Canal.

Squadron 100 Pipers were scrambled from Eilat to rescue Squadron 101 Commander Beni Peled. Piper pilot Gideon Finkelstein reported:

Flew for six minutes near Sharm El Sheikh when encountered enemy fire; nine rounds hit the fuel reservoir and fuel spilled in cockpit; switched tanks and landed at El Tor.

Piper 50 suffered CAT2 damage. Finkelstein indicated that the Piper was hit at 1445 while the Squadron 100 diary noted that 0450 was hit at 1545; the fact that Piper 50 diverted to El Tor and landed there may indicate that the hit was at 1545. Squadron 100 Technical Flight subsequently indicated:

A magnificent example of Piper endurance! A round entered cockpit, hit reserve fuel reservoir, penetrated firewall, entered electrical box and smashed at a magneto axis... The magneto continued to function normally and the Piper then flew for six hours, until arrival at Ramla, without a hitch.

Piper 50 was one of at least three Pipers that scanned Sharm

Squadron 103 operated ILAF C-47s, recruited Arkia C-47s and loaned French C-47s. The illustrated example is most likely a loaned French C-47.

Previously, the ILDF evaluated the strength of the EGDF Sharm El Sheikh sector garrison at a battalion; a battalion that was clearly fighting back as Egyptian fire hit six ILAF aircraft over the Sharm El Sheikh sector on 2 November: Mystère 84 and P-51 73 were shot down; B-17 1623, Mystère 52, P-51 53 and Piper 50 RTBed. By the end of the day, three C-47s were on the way to drop a small force at the Sharm El Sheikh sector. A Squadron 117 Meteor was therefore tasked to catch up the slower C-47s, convey orders to abandon the drop at Sharm El Sheikh and join the drop at El Tor.

El Sheikh's surrounding area in the search for Squadron 101 Commander. Beni Peled reported:

> I ran and walked for about 45 minutes, climbing in a gorge. I climbed in gorge until I located a shadowed place that was hidden from [Ras Nasrani] camp. I then inspected [myself] and what I had. I felt that my right ankle was wounded [actually broken] and that my left knee was sprained. I had cigarettes, matches, a sleeve and a pistol with two magazines. I then noted that I lost my knife and that my eyelashes and hairs on my hands were burnt [off]. I waited until it was getting dark and then I crawled to the foot of the mountains. I stayed in an area that was not seen from the [Ras Nasrani] camp. When the Pipers arrived, I waved the sleeve and the third Piper pinpointed me, landed, the scout and the pilot [Abraham Greenbaum] evacuated me [to the aircraft] and we took off.

SUPPORT BRIGADE 11

1515–	117	Meteor	Yoeli	support Bde 11
1515–	117	Meteor	Sapir	ditto
1515–1555	117	3604	Kaspit	ditto
1515–1555	117	3605	Yahalom	ditto

DROP EL TOR

1530–1900	103	1403	Shalev/Dvir/ Eyal/Alon	Drop El Tor
1530–1900	103	1420	Ohad/Rom/ Ashkenazi/Meir	ditto
1530–1900	103	1405	Oz/Shabty/Goldreich/ Strasman	ditto
1530–1900	103	1414	Ganot/Machnes/ Aloni/Cohen	ditto
1531–	103	C-47	Amrami	drop Sharm El Sheikh
1531–	103	C-47	Bliman	ditto
1531–1911	103	1412	Shamir/Michaeli	ditto
1610–	117	Meteor	Lavon	relay

The ILDF pressed ahead with the plan to drop paratroopers at El Tor and Sharm El Sheikh, regardless of information that the ILDF evaluation concerning the EGDF retreat from Sharm El Sheikh was incorrect.

TO BIR HAMA AND EL ARISH

	2815	Hashiloni/Gazit	Tel Nof–El Arish– Tel Nof	
1650–	117	3735	Zivoni	support Bde 11
1650–1720	117	3737	Sarig	ditto
1650–	117	Meteor	Altman	ditto
1650–	117	Meteor	Gat	ditto
1700–1730	116	2338	Eyal	support Bde 11
1700–	116	P-51	Burstein	ditto
1700–	116	P-51	Hasson	support Bde 11
1700–	116	P-51	Naveh	ditto

Divisions 38 and 77 advanced, so the supporting Squadron 100 flights were relocated to Bir Hama and El Arish, respectively. Fighting in the Khan Yunes sector continued, with Squadron 116 and Squadron 117 support; Mordechai Lavon, on his way back from retasking the Squadron 103 C-47s, also attacked.

AIRLIFT EL TOR

	103	1402	Biran/Vossman	Tel Nof–El Tor–Tel Nof
	103	1403	Shalev/Rom/Eyal	ditto
	103	1405	Oz/Shabty/ Strasman	ditto
	103	1412	Shamir/ Michaeli	ditto

AIR3 Isaiah Gazit flew to El Arish on 2 November 1956, in Consul 15, along with Achiya Hashiloni, where he was photographed in front of an abandoned EGAF Sokol.

103	ALH	Ben Josef/	ditto	
		Reubeni/Zioni/Nimrod		
	El Al	L-049	Tohar	ditto
110	2168	Orli/Levy	relay	

Squadron 103 pilot Michael Ben-Josef flew Noratlas 4X-ALH to El Tor during an airlift on the night of 2 to 3 November 1956. Noratlas 4X-FAP was painted as 4X-ALH for a pre-war clandestine mission and was not repainted in time for the Suez War.

Squadron 147 T-17s operated from Ramla - beside ILAF HQ - and flew mail and passengers between ILAF bases. Squadron 147 Meir Sheffer recalled:
'Squadron 147 pilots were mostly reserves plus air cadets from final phase of flying course... Squadron 147 missions were mostly transport between ILAF bases; we transported passengers and mail... Only pilots were issued with parachutes due to shortage... There was blackout and our aircraft's only navigation aide was a compass, so pilots flew along a heading and after calculated time of arrival started to circle over supposed base position while closing and opening throttle so that the local control tower would turn on runway lights. All nighttime flights were accomplished without a hitch thanks to high level of competence in instruments flying. There was no electrical runway lighting system at Ramla so we had a special team that was on duty to light up goosenecks before landing and to put out goosenecks after landings. In order to make sure that pilots would pinpoint Ramla, I ordered to keep one gooseneck on throughout all night, every night, and the gooseneck team was also in charge of putting out this single gooseneck in case of an alert. This gooseneck was practically the only light on in Israel during the blackout nights.

		110	2169	Levin
		Hatzor–Ramat David		
1900	69	1621		
		Lod–Ramat David		
2330	147	2713	Engel	
		Ramla, accident during take-off, CAT4		

Battalion 88 paratroopers occupied El Tor airfield and secured the locality for an airlift that transported Runway Branch Unit 810 – in a Noratlas from Lod – and Battalion 112 from Tel Nof. In his post-war report, Runway Branch Unit 810 Commander Shlomo Carmel noted:

> Runway [Branch] Unit 820 [typo, 810] was organized at Lod on 2 November and deployed to El Tor. Equipment supplied at Lod included: communication sets, generators, batteries, tools, fuels and general unit gear. Weight of equipment and 18 soldiers was heavier than allowed weight for a Noratlas. I was forced to leave at Lod the generators and cables for runway lights. The runway [at El Tor] was therefore marked with goosenecks throughout the night, thus risking aircraft and [potentially] revealing runway to enemy.

Day 6
3 NOVEMBER 1956

Brigades 7 and 27 approached the Suez Canal along SPINACH and RADISH, respectively. Brigade 4 replaced Brigade 202 at JAMAICA. Brigade 11 was occupying the Gaza Strip. Brigade 9 was still tasked to occupy Sharm El Sheikh. Brigade 202 was tasked to occupy Ras Sudar, link-up with El Tor and back-up the occupation of Sharm El Sheikh.

AIR4 INTELLIGENCE REPORT NUMBER 18

	103	FAQ	Thor/Kohen
		Tel Nof–El Tor–Tel Nof	
0215–0400	100A	0437	Milman/scout
		Ramla–Ramla, patrol Jordan	
0500–	100	Piper	Even/scout
		support Brigade 202	

Issued at 0030, AIR4 Intelligence Report Number 18 still repeated the inaccurate ILDF evaluation that the EGDF retreated from Sharm El Sheikh:

> Part of force deployed at Sharm El Sheikh sector had been evacuated by EGNF warship that sailed in direction of Suez. Remaining force had been concentrated at Ras Nasrani and had probably departed on its way to Suez during night. All positions at Sharm El Sheikh are empty.

However, the EGDF garrison did not retreat from Sharm El Sheikh and, for this reason, the ILDF retasked C-47s from the drop at Sharm El Sheikh to drop at El Tor some eight hours prior to the issue of AIR4 report. Additionally, AIR4 summed up estimated enemy losses

Squadron 100 Flight D Piper 31 was reportedly photographed on a road - presumably BENCH - near El Tor on 3 November 1956.

until then: out of 45,000 EGDF troops present in Sinai at the start of the war, some 17,000 were captured or killed; the ILDF and ILAF hit 45–50 tanks, but some of these were repairable; 15 tanks were captured intact. Squadron 100 pilot Moshe Even reported:

I took off to El Tor, with Major Dov from paratroopers, for coordination with force that landed there during night. On our way [to El Tor] we contacted force that was advancing to oil fields at Ras Sudar and force commander [Battalion 890 Commander Rafael Eitan] asked us to guide him over there and to recce the place. We recced [Ras Sudar] and informed him that the place was empty of military forces. We guided him to key areas until the place was occupied. We also guided them in direction of vehicles that were moving from north to south so that they would not report that ILDF was over there. In another case we stopped, with Uzi fire from back seat, two buses travelling south. After the place had been occupied, we headed to El Tor. We recced road [to ElTor], pinpointed places of interest and reported to force commander at El Tor.

OCCUPATION KHAN YUNES

0800–0855	113	4029	Sheffer	support Bde 11
0800–	113	Ouragan	Erez	ditto
	113	4047	Agassi	support Bde 11

The first pair attacked but the ILDF noted, at 0900, that Brigade 11 had occupied Khan Yunes so the second pair was called back and RTBed after 20 minutes in the air.

CASEVAC DAHAB

	103	1402	Biran/Vossman	
			Tel Nof–El Tor–Tel Nof	
	103	1405	Oz/Barkai/Goldreich/	
			Strasman	ditto
	103	1407	Kohen/Dvir	ditto
	103	1416	Avisar/Rom	
			Tel Nof–El Tor–JAMAICA–El Arish–	
			Tel Nof	
	103	FAR	Ben Josef/Lahav/Zioni/Nimrod	
			Tel Nof–El Arish–Tel Nof	
	110	2117	Orli	test, Haifa–Ramat David
	115	0473	Tavor	test

Squadron 113 pilot Samuel Sheffer flew Ouragan 29 to support Brigade 11 on the morning of 3 November 1956.

Squadron 113 Deputy A Jacob Agassi was scrambled in Ouragan 47 to support Brigade 11 on 3 November 1956 but was recalled and did not attack.

Squadron 103 pilot Michael Ben-Josef flew Noratlas 4X-FAR to El Arish during daylight on 3 November 1956.

	115	1173	Tavor	test
	115	2178	Tavor	test
	115	2190	Tavor	test
	147	2736	Shahar	Ramla–Lod–Ramla
0845–1000	100A	0450	Britstein	patrol Jordan

Restrictions upon daylight flying of transport aircraft were lifted and Squadron 103 airlifters flew to El Tor, Bir Hama, El Arish and JAMAICA. Brigade 9 encountered the enemy at Dahab, some 80 kilometers from Sharm El Sheikh, and the ILDF noted, at 0930, a signal from Brigade 9 that Dahab had been occupied. Squadron 100 Flight D Commander Isaac Hirsh reported:

Two soldiers reported on 1 November; they presented themselves as Brigade 9 scouts and said that they would scout with us for Brigade 9. Previously, I was not informed that we would have to cooperate with Brigade 9. The brigade started to advance south during evening on 1 November; that

Squadron 101 pilot Amos Lapidot flew Mystère 83 on 3 November 1956 – the only thus far unearthed sortie for 4583 during the Suez War. It was reportedly photographed during the Suez War while having its guns' ammunition boxes loaded.

night we flew two patrols and the following day we patrolled throughout the day. Our tasking was to communicate between vanguard and main body as well as to deliver vital stuff. Today, 3 November, the vanguard and the brigade arrived at Dahab, where a battle ensued between our forces and an enemy outpost; as a result, four were killed and five were injured. We landed at Dahab and evacuated all casualties to Eilat.

SEARCH FOR SHIP IN RED SEA

0940–1105	115	3518	Livneh/Sivron		
		Kaf19 photograph Jordan			
1115–1215	117	Meteor	Yoeli	support Bde 11	
1115–1215	117	Meteor	Sapir	ditto	
1115–1215	117	Meteor	Altman	ditto	
1115–1215	117	Meteor	Gat	ditto	
	117	3735	Zivoni	support Brigade 11	
	117	3731	Sarig	ditto	
1135–1255	100A	0402	Kos/scout	patrol	
		(terrorists north of Gaza Strip)			
1245–1705	110	Mosquito Fuchs/Bar Shalom			
		reconnaissance Red Sea			
1410–1550	115	3517	Livneh/Dim		
		Kaf20 photograph Syrian airfields,			
		landed at Ramat David			
1410–1605	117	3605	Yahalom escort Kaf20		
1425–1540	101gold1	4536	Avneri	reconnaissance	
				Sharm El Sheikh	
1425–1540	101gold2	4583	Lapidot ditto		

The ILDF noted, at 0945, a Brigade 202 report that Ras Sudar had been occupied. At 1045, the ILDF noted a report that Brigade 9 initiated advance in direction of Ras Nasrani. At 1100, air support requests from Brigades 9 and 11 were noted.

Squadron 117 Meteors were scrambled to support Brigade 11, but none attacked. The four-ship formation was vectored to the Khan Yunes sector but did not attack due to the presence of civilians and was retasked to look for ships, but none was observed; the pair was tasked to pinpoint an Egyptian submarine supposedly off the Gaza Strip, but found nothing and was vectored to Khan Yunes but did not attack due to the presence of civilians.

At 1123, the ILDF noted a report from Brigade 202 that Mitle Pass was not in Israeli hands and that an aerial patrol was dispatched to check if enemy forces were still at Mitle Pass. At 1130, Piper 59 suffered CAT2 damage during an exchange of fire between ILDF guards and EGDF troops at El Arish airfield. At 1145, the ILDF noted that a Battalion 88 company had started to advance from El Tor to Sharm El Sheikh.

Brigade 9 ALO Elijah Rosen stated that listening revealed that a ship with 600 troops was on its way to reinforce Sharm El Sheikh, so Brigade 9 ALO reported this information over FAC radio network and requested that the ship be attacked. It is not known when this request was forwarded, but a Squadron 110 Mosquito recced the Red Sea. Yigal Bar Shalom recalled:

> By the time of the Suez War I was no longer a Squadron 115 navigator, I was an AIR4 staff officer so only after several days was I finally granted permission to fly [a mission]. Fuchsi and me flew alone along [Saudi coastline] to look for EGNF that reportedly fled to Saudi Arabia. We flew an overwhelming flight at low altitude, along the coastline, down to Red Sea... It was a fascinating flight.

At about the same time, Squadron 101's gold section pinpointed an unidentified ship near Sharm El Sheikh.

ASSAULT MITLE PASS?

1525–1645	100A	0421	Rachman/scout	patrol	
Jordan					
1545–1835	115	3518	Eyal/Galon	Kaf23	
photograph PortTaufik					

Brigade 202 reported, at 1500, that an air patrol concluded that Mitle Pass was empty of enemy forces, so the brigade planned an evening assault. AIR1 ordered, at 1515, the closure of Runway Branch Unit 322 and 731; Runway Unit 721 was to replace Runway Branch Unit 322 as operator of El Arish airfield.

STRIKE SHIP

1545–1835	116	2370	Yavneh	
		attack ship in Red Sea		
1545–	116	P-51	Burstein	ditto
1545–	116	P-51	Hativa	ditto
1545–	116	P-51	Rafaeli	ditto
1545–1835	116	2312	Barak	ditto
1545–	116	P-51	Bloch	ditto
1545–	116	P-51	Sharon	ditto
1545–	116	P-51	Kohorn	ditto
	115	3517	Livneh/Dim	
		Ramat David–Tel Nof		
1618–1735	101white1	4560	Bar	
		attack ship in Red Sea		
1618–1735	101white2	4590	Bet On	ditto
1618–1735	101white3	4529	Gilboa	ditto
1618–1735	101white4	4562	Margalit	ditto
1623–1740	101red1	4552	Shapira	
		attack ship in Red Sea		
1623–1740	101red2	4546	Harel	ditto
1623–1740	101red3	4528	Gonen	ditto

Squadron 116 Deputy A Dan Barak flew P-51 12 in lead of a four-ship formation tasked to strike a ship in the Red Sea on 3 November 1956. The P-51s were in common configuration for interdiction with six rockets and two napalm canisters - as P-51 on right is configured - while bombs - such as the one on the trolley - might have been more effective against a warship.

101red4   4549   Dekel
ditto, didn not take off

Apparently, Squadron 101 Mystères and a Squadron 110 Mosquito pinpointed a ship that matched the reported message of the plan to reinforce Sharm El Sheikh, so eight Mystères and eight P-51s were tasked to strike the ship. Two P-51s aborted the mission en route and RTBed; one Mystère malfunctioned before take-off. Squadron 101 white rocketed a ship and Squadron 101 red rocketed a warship. Dan Barak recalled:

> We saw a frigate in the Red Sea; it was at about 1700; eight aircraft with napalm and rockets. I was in contact with Dani Shapira of the Mystères; I asked if he knows something about this frigate [and Shapira replied] 'I do not know; it is not supposed to be here; we already attacked it; attack it too!'. I was not in contact with ILAF HQ so we attacked but I realized very quickly that it was not an Egyptian frigate,[due to] the amount of AAA fire, like fireworks, red, green, there was a tremendous AAA barrage. Napalm is not a suitable weapon [to strike ships]; to drop it you had to come very low; we all missed. We attacked with rockets; two rockets hit.

The warship was indeed not Egyptian; it was HMS Crane, which suffered very light damage. Amnon Bloch recalled:

> We arrived at about 8,000 feet... and while diving we were supposed to launch rockets, change setting of ordnance selector and drop napalm. The aircraft accelerated to a very high speed, the ship opened [AAA] fire like a mushroom, a lot [of AAA fire] ... so [in order not to continue acceleration] I throttled back and recovered from dive. It was all quiet, getting dark and I did not see anyone... I opened throttle and looked for the others but saw nobody. Suddenly, I saw lights, an aircraft got closer and Zvi Kohorn said 'lead me home!'. Two aircraft flying in total darkness, not a single light was seen [on the ground] until we reached Beer Sheba; all ILAF was worried about us so all runway lights north of Teman Field were switched on and we landed at Hatzor with fuel gauges on zero.

AIR4 Intelligence Report Number 22, issued at 0030 on 4 November, stated:

> Our aircraft attacked and sunk an Egyptian ship that was evacuating troops from nearby Ras Nasrani. Our aircraft attacked an enemy destroyer nearby Sharm El Sheikh; the ship was damaged.

FROM SUNSET TO MIDNIGHT

	103	1416	Avisar/Eyal
		VIP Chief of Staff	
	103	1432	Shamir/Michaeli
		Tel Nof–JAMAICA–Tel Nof	
	117	3604	Kaspit
		Tel Nof–Ramat David	
1800–	103	C-47	Biham
		psywar Sharm El Sheikh	

Squadron 103 Commander flew the ILDF Chief of Staff to visit units in Sinai; Squadron 103 pilot Uri Biham dropped leaflets over the Sharm El Sheikh sector and, on the way back, landed at Eilat and evacuated casualties, including Squadron 101 Commander Beni Peled.

AIR4 Intelligence Report Number 21 was issued at 1730 and indicated a yet-to-be-confirmed message that a small number of EGAF Il-28s and MiGs retreated to Luxor. Concerning the situation at Sharm El Sheikh, the report stated:

> The Egyptian forces at Ras Nasrani are entrenching for defense.

AIR1 announced, at 1800, activation of ILAF Survey Unit 177 with Emanuel Giladi as commander and Jacob Nevo as the only other pilot in the team of mostly ordnance experts that was tasked to survey Sinai in order to evaluate the effectiveness of ILAF operations.

Day 7
4 NOVEMBER 1956

The ILDF completed the occupation of Sinai except for a strip east of the Suez Canal and the Sharm El Sheikh sector. Squadron 103 flew ILDF HQ officers to get in contact with Brigade 9 for a first-hand impression of the situation. While the Squadron 103 aircraft was in the air, the ILDF issued a series of orders all aimed to expedite the occupation of Sharm El Sheikh:

– At 0015, Brigade 9 reported that scouts encountered enemy en route to Ras Nasrani.

– At 0015, the ILDF ordered that Brigade 202's Battalion 890 would advance to Sharm El Sheikh via El Tor and would then be attached to Brigade 9 for the actual occupation of Sharm El Sheikh.

– At 0100, the ILDF ordered that Brigade 202's Battalion 88 company at El Tor – which reportedly initiated the advance to Sharm El Sheikh but then returned to El Tor – would be attached to Battalion 890, while Brigade 12's Battalion 112 would remain at El Tor.

AIR4 INTELLIGENCE REPORT NUMBER 18

0530–0655   101blue1 4594   Morgan Kaf24
reconnaissance Jordan/Syria

Flight 124 was practically opened on 4 November when Squadron 103 pilot Judah Arbel and Flight 124 Commander Uri Yarom transferred the two S-55 helicopters from Tel Nof - where AMU22 had just completed assembly of the helicopters - to Ramla, from where Flight 124 was planned to operate as a Squadron 100 subordinated unit.

0530–0655	101blue2	4591	Zuk	ditto
	103	1420	BenJosef/Reubeni/Zioni/Bass	
			Tel Nof–El Tor–Tel Nof	
	110	2123	Proshanski	
			Kfar Sirkin–Ramat David	
	115	2139	Tavor	test
	115	2178	Tavor	test
	115	3515	Eyal/Sivron	
			test camera over Sinai	
	124	S-55	Arbel	Tel Nof–Ramla
	124	S-55	Yarom	Tel Nof–Ramla
	147	2739	Benjamini/Shahar	
			Ramat David–Ramla	
	147	2748	Kamil/Shahar	
			Ramla–Kfar Sirkin–Megiddo–Ramat David	
	147	2755	Markman/Shahar	
			Ramla–Tel Nof–Hatzor–Teman Field–Ramla	
	0472		Tavor	test
	0473		Tavor	test

MIOR Kaf24's tasking was to collect information concerning the alleged deployment to Jordan of an Iraqi expeditionary force. The Mysteres were tasked to fly to Ramat David, thence over the road across Jordan to Iraq and to recce on the way back. MIOR indicated an altitude of 37,000 feet during the flight to the target but any altitude suitable for visual reconnaissance over the target, which was practically most of the route. AIR4 reported:

> Some 70–80 vehicles were spotted between H-3 and H-4, including 25 armored vehicles and Jeeps and 10 trucks towing guns.

LUXOR RAID 1

AIR4 Intelligence Report Number 23, issued at 0600, claimed that the EGAF still had 27–34 serviceable Il-28s, of which about 20 had been flown to Saudi Arabia. At 0552, 13 Squadron 200 F-84Fs departed Lod to raid Luxor, about 300 kilometers from Sharm El Sheikh, where EGAF Il-28s and MiGs reportedly sought refuge from Anglo-French attacks, while the presence of Il-28s and MiGs at Luxor also potentially endangered the ILDF at Sharm El Sheikh.

FRIENDLY FIRE RAS NASRANI?

0750–	110		Mosquito Somech	support Bde 9
0750–1145	110	2177	Proshanski/	ditto
			Bar Shalom	
0750–	110		Mosquito Bavli	ditto
0750–	110		Mosquito Amiran	ditto
0820–1140	110	2168	Orli/	support Bde 9
			Levy	
0820–	110		Mosquito Landau	ditto
0820–1055	110	2167	Levin/Davidson	ditto
0820–	110	2184	Shemer	ditto

Contrary to ILDF/I evaluation, the EGDF retreated from Ras Nasrani and concentrated forces at Sharm El Sheikh. The ILAF renewed suppression of the Sharm El Sheikh sector in preparation for Brigade 9 or Brigade 202 attack; the first to attack were Squadron 110 Mosquitoes. IOKR stated:

> Aircraft attacked Ras Nasrani (after occupation by our forces) and Sharm El Sheikh but in both places did not detect any enemy activity.

However, Mosquito pilots Dave Orli, Amity Levin, Haim Proshanski and Amram Shemer all reported that the tasking was to attack Sharm El Sheikh; Orli and Levin indeed attacked Sharm El Sheikh, while Levin and Shemer did not attack because en route to Sharm El Sheikh a cockpit window detached from 2167, so Levin aborted the mission and RTBed with wingman Shemer as escort.

Moreover, the ILDF noted only at 1200 a Brigade 9 report that Ras Nasrani had been occupied – without a battle as the area had been deserted – so IOKR's implication of a 'friendly fire' possibility between Squadron 110 and Brigade 9 at Ras Nasrani is highly unlikely.

SHARM EL SHEIKH DESERTED?

| 0830–1425 | 69#2 | 1622) | Narunski | as follows |
| 0840–1425 | 69#1 | 1621 | Ben Haim/Efrat | support Bde 9 |

Squadron 69 servicemen in front of B-17 21 parked in a pen at Ramat David; 1621 was delivered to Squadron 69 on the evening of 2 November 1956 and flew a mission on 4 November 1956.

0920–1040	100A	0490	Rachman	patrol Jordan
1015–1135	115	3517	Livneh/Galon Kaf25 photograph Jordan	
1020–	116	P-51	Hasson	support Bde 9
1020–	116	P-51	Naveh	ditto
1020–	116	2337	Sharon	ditto
1020–	116	P-51	Cohen	ditto

The B-17s were tasked to bomb Ras Nasrani, but 15 minutes prior to take-off the target was changed to Sharm El Sheikh. When Reuben Narunski arrived over the target he was notified by Squadron 116 P-51 pilots and Squadron 110 Mosquito crews that Sharm El Sheikh was deserted. Narunski called Central Control Unit for orders but was unable to make contact, so he orbited over Sharm El Sheikh, waiting for Jacob Ben Haim to arrive. While orbiting, Narunski photographed the target area and noted troops west of Sharm El Sheikh. The B-17 crew could not tell if these troops were Egyptian or Israeli, and it was impossible to contact Brigade 9 ALO in order to discuss this issue. After Ben Haim arrived, the two bombers attempted to bomb Sharm El Sheikh as planned but the bombs of 1621 did not drop. Ben Haim tried another bombing run and again the bombs did not drop, so they flew a third run and jettisoned bombs in emergency mode; the bombs were released but did not hit the target.

After the B-17s returned to Ramat David and the photos were analyzed, the troops were identified as Egyptian; possibly the first proof that Sharm El Sheikh had not been deserted.

LUXOR RAID 2

Taken by FRAF RF-84F, operating from Cyprus, probably at 1205, these BDA images of Luxor revealed 17 destroyed Il-28s - marked in circles, some still smoking - plus one - marked in rectangle - seemingly intact. If indeed taken at 1205, then these were all destroyed by Squadron 200's first wave attack. Since Squadron 200's first wave pilots reported some 25 Il-28s and one MiG, it is possible that all still serviceable aircraft were flown away between the departure of attacking F-84Fs and the arrival of photographing RF-84F.

AIR4 Intelligence Report Number 24, issued at 1115, stated:

> A French fighter-bomber squadron departed during early morning hours to strafe Luxor airfield. Some 25 Il-28s and one MiG were observed. Initial evaluation indicated that 10 Il-28s were destroyed, others were damaged and one bomber managed to take-off and escaped. No AAA was encountered.

In light of this evaluation, the majority of Il-28s at Luxor were not destroyed so a second wave of six Squadron 200 F-84Fs, tasked to raid Luxor, departed Lod at 1120.

P-51S ATTACK SHARM EL SHEIKH

1215–1525	105	2369	Bodilewski support Bde 9	
1215–1540	105	2354	Niv	ditto
1215–	105	P-51	Hagani OR Shaked	ditto
1215–1440	105	2331	Magen	ditto
	110	2168	Orli/Levy Tel Nof–Ramat David	
1310–1410	115	3517	Livneh/Raviv Kaf26 photograph Jordan	
1525–1915	116	2330	Barak support Bde 9	
1525–	116	P-51	Bloch	ditto
1525–	116	P-51	Hativa	ditto
1525–	116	P-51	Rafaeli	ditto
1530–1630	100A	0490	Milman/photographer photograph Jordan	

IOKR indicated that Squadron 105 pilots attacked between Sharm El Sheikh and Ras Nasrani, and that Squadron 116 supported Brigade 9's scout unit during an attack against an Egyptian outpost, while Dan Barak reported:

> Napalm, rockets and strafing on port of Sharm El Sheikh.

SINAI CIRCUIT TASKING

1551 –	103		
ALH FAP	Ofer/Kohen/Saul/		

Tel Nof–El Tor–Tel Nof Nimrod

The ILDF noted, at 1700, a Brigade 9 position report, five kilometers from Sharm El Sheikh; Squadron 103 indicated, at 1820, that fuel for Brigade 9 had been dropped some eight kilometers from Sharm El Sheikh; 1401 and/or 1402 were

Squadron 100 Commander Michael Keren reported Pipers' position at 2045 on 4 November 1956:
- Beer Sheba 0440 0445 0446 0453 0454 0455 0466 0467 0492
- Division 38 0438 0451
- Division 77 0447 (probably typo) 0471
- Brigade 9 0431 0448
- Brigade 202 0450 0456
- Eilat HQ 0452

forced to land at El Arish due to malfunction. At 2305, Squadron 103 reported a new tasking: a Sinai circuit. Daniel Rosin's crew was the first tasked to fly a Sinai circuit, with take-off scheduled at 1000 on 5 November, and the route Tel Nof–Eilat–Sharm El Sheikh–HOLOLULU–JAMAICA–Bir Hama–El Arish–Tel Nof. Obviously, at the time, Sharm El Sheikh was not yet in ILDF hands.

Day 8
5 NOVEMBER 1956

Brigade 9 assaulted Sharm El Sheikh during night of 4 to 5 November, but at 0330 the ILDF noted that the attack failed so Brigade 9 waited for daytime to attack again with ILAF support.

ENEMY AIRCRAFT OVER SHARM EL SHEIKH?

	103	1404	Oz/Shabty/Goldreich	
			Tel Nof–El Tor–Tel Nof	
	103	1407	Biran/Amrami	
			drop fuel to Bde 9	
	103	1409	Sela/Biham/Judah/Bok	
			Tel Nof–(El Tor) –Tel Nof	
	103	ALH FAP	Ofer/Kohen/Saul/	
			Tel Nof–El Tor–Tel Nof	Nimrod
0530–0650	101blue1	4594	Morgan	Kaf24
			reconnaissance Jordan/Syria	
0530–0650	101blue2	4591	Zuk	ditto
0550–0840	116	2343	Barak	
			support Bde 9	
0550–	116	2345	Fredilis	ditto
0550–	116	P-51	Hasson	ditto
0550–	116	P-51	Burstein	ditto
0700–0810	101	4564	Alon	
	black1		support Bde 9	
0700–0810	101	4563	Dekel	ditto
	black2			

Squadron 101 pilot Uri Dekel flew Mystère 63 as black 2 on the morning of 5 November 1956.

0720–0845	101	4547	Shadmi	
	green1		support Brigade 9	
0720–0845	101	4560	Ronen	ditto
	green2			
0725–1020	115	Meteor		Kaf27
		photograph Jordan/Syria		

Squadron 101 repeated MIOR Kaf24 and Squadron 115 flew MIOR Kaf27 to monitor the alleged deployment to Jordan of an Iraqi expeditionary force, but the ILAF's Day 8 focal point was Sharm El Sheikh. The first formation tasked to support Brigade 9 did not receive a MIOR but was scrambled. Dan Barak reported:

> Called [Central] Control [Unit] and was ordered to proceed to Sharm El Sheikh and to beware of enemy aircraft over target. I asked for type of aircraft, piston or jet, and was answered that this was not known. I asked if there would be a cover of our jet aircraft over target and was answered that this was taken care [of].
> En route to target, when we were 20 miles north of Eilat, Number 3 reported strong engine vibrations and that he was about to land at Eilat. The pilot jettisoned napalm over empty desert and landed at Eilat with rockets...... The aircraft is still there [at the time of debrief, 1410].
> Over target I contacted [Brigade 9] ALO [Elijah Rosen] who told me to contact FAC Joshua [Nachman] … I saw FAC Mobile half-track and he guided me to attack bunkers... I saw two bunkers on a hill, about 300 meters north of camp, dropped two napalm canisters on the bunkers and noted good hits and explosions, possibly exploding ammunition inside bunkers. I strafed and rocketed fortifications on both sides of main road to camp in line with ALO directives. I then strafed targets in line with orders from FAC Joshua until I finished ammunition; these targets did not return fire. Number 2 and 4 followed me [throughout the attack]. On our way back we were forced to land at Eilat in order to refuel.

The P-51s attacked at 0715 so the Mysteres probably arrived a little later; both pairs patrolled over Sharm El Sheikh, and Squadron 101's green section also strafed.

OCCUPATION SHARM EL SHEIKH

0835–	116	P-51	Zeelon	
			support Bde 9	
0835–	116	P-51	Bloch	ditto
0835–	116	2337	Sharon	ditto

Squadron 140 returned from Teman Field to Tel Nof on 5 November 1956. Walking in front of a T-6 line at Tel Nof - still equipped with rockets racks - is Flying School instructor Shlomo Erez, who was on emergency posting to Squadron 113 Ouragan during the Suez War.

0835–	116	P-51	Kohorn	ditto
0845–1115	100A	0450	Milman/scout	patrol Jordan
0915–1010	101 khaki1	4542	Lev support Bde 9	
0915–1010	101 khaki2	4580	Gur	ditto
0935–1105	101 yellow1	4552	Gonen support Bde 9	
0935–1105	101 yellow2	4544	Zuk	ditto

The P-51s flew one attack pass, were called off and later jettisoned their remaining napalm canisters over the sea; at 0945, the ILDF noted a Brigade 9 message that Sharm El Sheikh was in Israeli hands.

RETURN TO PEACETIME

	103	1428	Thor/Rom	
			Tel Nof–El Tor–HONOLULU–Tel Nof	
	110	2117	Levin/Segal	test
	115	2139	Tavor	test
	115	2190	Tavor	test
	115	3518	Livneh	test

	116	2303	Fredilis	test
	140	1140	Nachman	
			Teman Field–Tel Nof	
	140	1144	Gideoni	ditto
	147	2753	Shahar	
			Ramla–Kfar Sirkin–Megiddo–Ramat David–Ramla	
	147	2753	Sheffer	Tel Nof–Ramla
	147	2755	Sheffer	Ramla–Tel Nof
		0472	Tavor	test
		0474	Tavor	test
1030–	103	1402	Rosin/Vedeles/Strasman	
			Sinai circuit Tel Nof–Eilat–El Tor–JAMAICA–Bir Hama–El Arish–Tel Nof	
1120–1205	101gold1	4542	Avneri	
			patrol Gaza–El Arish	
1120–1205	101gold2	4562	Lapidot	ditto
1230–	103	1426	Shamir/Michaeli	
			Tel Nof–Sharm El Sheikh–Tel Nof CASEVAC	
1605 –	103	1432	Biran/Amrami	
			Tel Nof–JAMAICA–Tel Nof	
	103	1405	Lee/Kohen	
			Tel Nof–JAMAICA–Tel Nof	

The ILAF's return for peacetime practice was initiated. Squadron 140 returned to Tel Nof, the first phase in preparation for the restart of training flights that had been suspended prior to war.

Day 9
6 NOVEMBER 1956

	69	1621	Efrat/Josefon	test
	103	1405	Ofer/Kohen/Saul/Nimrod	
			Kaf36 VIP ILDF Chief of Staff	
			Tel Nof–Sharm El Sheikh–Tel Nof	
	103	1418	Rosin/Vedeles/Strasman	
			Tel Nof–Sharm El Sheikh	
	103	1420	Oz/Shabty/Goldreich	
			Kaf37	
	103	1428	Rosin/Vedeles/Strasman	
			Sharm El Sheikh–Ras Sudar–Sharm El Sheikh–El Tor–Eilat–Tel Nof	
	103	1430	BenJosef/Reubeni/Zioni/Bass	
			Tel Nof–Eilat–Tel Nof	
	117	3515	Sarig	Tel Nof–Ramat David
	117	3518	Yahalom	Tel Nof–Ramat David
	117	3603	Kaspit	Tel Nof–Ramat David
	117	3604	Yahalom	Tel Nof–Ramat David
	117	3606	Sarig	Tel Nof–Ramat David
	117	3735	Zivoni	Tel Nof–Ramat David

Squadron 103 aircraft at Sharm El Sheikh, probably on 6 November 1956.

	147	2731	Shahar	
		Ramla–Kfar Sirkin–Megiddo–Ramat David–Ramla		
	147	2736	Shahar	Ramla–Tel Nof
	1128	Ruff/Oren		Tel Nof–El Arish–Bir Hama–Tel Nof
	2815	Tavor/Livneh		Tel Nof–El Arish–Tel Nof
0910	100	0492	Gordon/Simhoni	
		Beer Sheba - Sharm El Sheikh		
1300 –1800	100	0416	Rachman Ramla–El Arish–Ramla	
1547–1810	100	0467		El Arish–El Arish, patrol
1530–	100	0492	Gordon/Simhoni/Dromi	
		El Tor - (Beer Sheba)		
1600 –1800	100	0401	Shuef	Tel Nof–El Arish–Ramla
1610–1705	100	0471	Ophir	El Arish–El Arish, patrol
	103	1432	Biran/Richter	Kaf38
1900–	103	1403	Sela	Tel Nof–El Arish

The return to peacetime continued: Squadron 117 returned to Ramat David and Squadron 147 to Tel Nof. The ILDF Chief of Staff and Command South Commander visited Brigade 9 at Sharm El Sheikh; on the way back, Piper 92 crashed in the West Bank with the loss of Squadron 100 pilot Benjamin Gordon, Command South Commander Asaf Simhoni and his assistant.

Day 10
7 NOVEMBER 1956

	103	1416	Ofer/Nachman/Goldreich	
		Tel Nof–El Tor–Tel Nof		
	103	1418	Kohen/Portugali	
		Kaf41 Sinai circuit		
		Tel Nof–Sharm El Sheikh–El Tor–JAMAICA–Bir Hama–El Arish–Tel Nof		
	103	1424	Bliman/Sivron	Kaf42
	103	FAQ	BenJosef/Vossman/Zioni/Bass	
		Tel Nof–El Tor–Tel Nof		
	110	1110	Levin/Kislev	
		Ramat David–Tel Nof–Ramat David		
	110	2124	Orli	
		Kfar Sirkin–Tel Nof		
	110	2133	Proshanski	
		Kfar Sirkin–Tel Nof		
	110	2135	Orli	
		Kfar Sirkin–Tel Nof		
	110	2174	Orli	
		Kfar Sirkin–Lod		
	2816	Tavor		
		test then Tel Nof–Hatzor–Tel Nof		
0515 –	103	1426)	Oz/Shabty/Goldreich	
		drop (Ras Sudar)		

Brigade 9 end of war parade at Sharm El Sheikh on 6 November 1956, from left to right Command South Commander Asaf Simhoni, ILDF Chief of Staff Moshe Dayan and Brigade 9 Commander Abraham Yoffe; sometime later Asaf Simhoni departed Sharm El Sheikh in Squadron 100 Piper 92.

Day 11
8 NOVEMBER 1956

Time	Sqn	A/C	Pilot	Route
0600–	100	0449	Aaroni	Beer Sheba–El Arish
0630–0945	100	0471	Ophir	El Arish–Tel Nof–El Arish
0900–	100	0467	Cooperman	El Arish–El Arish, patrol
0900–	100	0473		Ramla–El Arish
0940–	1001	0474	(Salmon)	Ramla–El Arish
1050–1220	100	0449	Aaroni	El Arish–El Arish
1050–	100	0471	Ophir	El Arish–El Arish
1100	2811		Kafri	Tel Nof–El Arish–Bir Hama–Bir Gafgafa–El Tor–El Arish–Tel Nof
1105–	100	0440	Kadmon	Teman Field–El Arish–Dov Field
1105–	100	0446	Brosh	Teman Field–El Arish
1130–	100	0467	Cooperman	El Arish–El Arish, patrol
1300–	100	0449	Aaroni	El Arish–Beer Sheba
1300–	100	0467	Cooperman	El Arish–Beer Sheba
1300–	100	0471	Ophir	El Arish–Beer Sheba
1415–1615	100	0446	Brosh	El Arish–El Arish, patrol Suez Canal
1740–	100	0446	Brosh	El Arish–Beer Sheba
	103	1428	BenJosef/Bloch/Zioni/Alon	Tel Nof–Ramat David–Tel Nof
	2811		Tavor	Tel Nof–Lod–Ramat David–Tel Nof
	103	1404	Oz/Safra/Goldreich	Tel Nof–Abu Rhodes–Tel Nof
	0476		Tavor	test
0710–	100	0440	Kadmon	Dov Field–El Arish–Ramla–El Arish
0720–	124	4602	Arbel	Ramla–El Arish–JAMAICA–El Arish–Ramla
0720–	124	4603	Yarom	ditto
0840–1615	100	0446	Brosh	El Arish–El Tor–El Arish
0910–1510	100	0440	Kadmon	El Arish–Ramla–El Arish
0945–		2811	Tavor	Tel Nof–El Arish–Dov Field–Tel Nof
0950–	100	0473		El Arish–Bir Hama–Bir Gafgafa
1503–	103	1411	Biran/Ostashinski	Tel Nof–Abu Rhodes–Tel Nof
1600–1655	101	4552	Shadmi	patrol Suez Canal
1600–1655	101	4549	Golan	ditto
1640–2000	100	0440	Kadmon	El Arish–El Arish, patrol

AIR3 Operations Officer Isaiah Gazit signaled, at 1740, to ILAF units:

Ceasefire will be in force from acceptance of this order. Enemy targets will not be attacked outside territories in ILDF control, that is to say:

– Along Jordan, Lebanon and Syria frontiers the 1948 [actually 1949] Armistice lines.

– On Egyptian frontier Sinai Peninsula up to 15 kilometers east of Suez Canal.

A Squadron 103 Noratlas, reportedly at El Tor.